The Freshman Fabulous:

The Girl's Guide to College

by

Jessica Ekstrom

TELEMACHUS PRESS

Cover art and design by Lauren Hadeed

Published by Telemachus Press, LLC
http://www.telemachuspress.com

Visit the author's websites:
http://www.JessEkstrom.com
http://www.TheFreshmanFabulous.com
http://www.HeadbandsOfHope.org

ISBN: 978-1-941536-63-6 (eBook)
ISBN: 978-1-941536-67-4 (Paperback)

Version 2015.02.24

Printed in the United States of America

10 9 8 7 6 5 4 3 2 1

Written by a recent grad for the future grad.

Table of Contents

The Freshman Fabulous:

The Girl's Guide to College

Hey, I'm Jess!

I know what you're thinking. *"Who's this girl who thinks she knows all about college? Is she a professor? A college psychologist? Does a college psychologist even exist?"*

To answer your last question: I have no idea if a college psychologist exists. And therefore, you can infer that I'm not one.

To answer your first question: My name is Jessica Ekstrom (people usually call me Jess), and I'm a recent college graduate (class of 2013 all the way, baby). During college, I interned at Disney World, Make-A-Wish and the *TODAY Show*.

My internship at Make-A-Wish led me to create a company my junior year called Headbands of Hope. For every headband purchased, one is given to a girl with cancer and one dollar is donated to fund childhood cancer research. By the time I graduated, Headbands of Hope became my fulltime job and was rippling across the nation.

During college, I was a campus tour guide, a group fitness instructor and made Dean's List every semester. I won scholarships and received the *Role Model of the Year* award; I had competed among students throughout the entire university. The biggest honor I received was being chosen to give the commencement speech at my graduation to over 20,000 people.

Let me clarify two things …

1. Even though I had success in college, that's not what this book is about. It's about finding YOUR success.
2. It wasn't always this way.

In high school I was rarely recognized, except for sports. My sister was the president of the student body at our high school (well deserved) and always at the top of everything. I have zero bitterness towards her. She's hard-working and deserves everything she's received. But going into college, I was tired of being in the background. I didn't want to be referred to as "Heather's sister" anymore. I wanted to create my own identity.

So I decided to try to make those four years into "transformation" years and turn into the person I had always wanted to be. And I did.

I'm never going to be done transforming and growing, but my time and experiences in college definitely served as a launching pad in the direction I wanted to go.

Am I an expert? That depends how you define expert. Did I ever make mistakes? Of course, and continue to do so.

So why should you listen to me?

I have gained such a clear understanding of the impact college can make on a person, no matter what you study, how old you are or your background. It's a time to explore what you really want to know about and figure out how to get there.

Now that you know about me, let's talk about you …

Prologue

Let's start off by getting this thought out of your head: College is the best four years of your life. Play your cards right and you will have *many* wonderful experiences up until your last days: marrying the person you love, traveling to a new country, having kids, finding a discount on that dress you love, finally learning how to use a crock pot (I still don't know how to use one) and many, many more.

When you walk across the stage at graduation, there shouldn't be an overwhelming feeling of sadness thinking the best years of your life are over. The purpose of college is to prepare you to live the life you want. So even though graduation marks the end of college, it marks the beginning of a potentially amazing life, too.

But one very important aspect that's different about college is that you have one shot to make it count. Sure, there's grad school and such, but it isn't the same as undergrad.

So why not make the most of it?

Born--------------------/---------/--Die

Everything that happens between those two small lines above is college. Four years (or however long your undergrad is) might seem like a long time. However in the scope of your whole life, it's only a little tiny piece. And that piece will continue to affect the rest of that line.

It's important to note that I don't mean that you should do everything right during college. In fact, a lot of this book is about making mistakes. But it's what you do after you fail and how you react that will truly affect the rest of your life.

This book does not contain research, scientific studies or facts. It's just one college girl's opinions to another. Maybe you'll find something in here that changes your college career for the better. Maybe you'll find something you don't agree with. Maybe you'll find a really funny quote you'll tweet to all your friends. Whatever happens, I hope you enjoy the book.

So, now that you understand what this book is about, let's begin.

PART 1: SCHOOL

Picking a School

Stacy Nadeau, DePaul University, Class of 2007

I'll never forget sitting at my kitchen table on that fateful April night. It was the night before I had to turn in my college decision letter, and I was elbow deep in the trusty "pro/con" list. I was great at creating a long list of **logical** *positives and negatives about each place.*

I was choosing between two amazing schools in two large cities where I'd be moving far from home, not knowing a single person in either place. My anxiety was through the roof. So many thoughts were going through my head:

"This is a huge decision!"

"This will decide the course of my next four years and possibly my career."

"The city I pick will probably be where I get my first job, make new friends, and maybe meet my husband! Etc."

THE PRESSURE!

I agonized all night and hardly slept.

The next morning, I **had** *to make a decision. I was becoming more and more worked up when my mom turned to me and calmly said, "Just go with your gut."*

I snapped out of it. After taking a few deeps breaths, I threw out my logical list and I found "my gut." I picked a school, had an amazing four years, and loved every second of it.

I think about this moment often. I think about how I agonized and put so much pressure on myself to make the "perfect" or "right" decision.

It taught me to think about decisions differently. Now, I think of things as "trials," not end results. If you think about decisions as something "I'm just trying out," it relieves pressure and reminds you it is never too late to change your mind. There is always a chance to pivot and go in a new direction— hope is never lost!

There have been numerous times since then I've "tried" something and it didn't work. I learned from it and pivoted to something new. Trials are always learning experiences. Sometimes they work, sometimes they don't. Either way, trust in yourself you have the skills to pivot, try something else, and be successful.

Choosing a School

If you've already been accepted or are currently in school, I give you permission to skip to chapter two. Don't worry—I won't be offended.

I never had a dream school. I remember in high school when it was the "cool thing" to wear a UNC shirt or have a Harvard magnet on your locker because it was your first choice. I pretended to be a die-hard fan of any school, so when people would ask me, "What's your first choice?" I'd have something to say.

"Definitely University of Georgia, I hear they have a good football team and their dining halls don't suck."

That was all I could come up with.

I wasn't really sure what I wanted to do with my life so I didn't choose a school based on a certain major. I played volleyball, but I wasn't good enough to play at a big school, so I threw that in the can.

Naturally, I panicked. *How will I ever be good in college if I don't even know of even one school I want to go to?*

I applied to twelve different schools. Why? I have no idea. I swear, I couldn't pronounce the names of some of the schools where I applied. Maybe the brochure I got in the mail had a pretty picture on it?

As I started to get back acceptances (and plenty of denies), I came to a realization.

What qualities do I want in a school? Maybe I don't know one particular school that I want to go to, but I did know qualities that I was looking for in a college.

- I want to go to a BIG state school. I went to a small private school for high school where everyone knew what the other person had for lunch. It was time for a change.
- I wanted a school that focused more on the holistic student, not just grades and academics. To me, it's important to be recognized for involvement in your community, extra curricular activities, and hands-on experiences.
- A football team! My high school didn't have one. I never knew how much I was missing!
- I wanted a school in state for affordable tuition (and I just love North Carolina).

It all made perfect sense to me. Instead of finding one school and deciding it's your "first choice," find multiple schools that have the qualities you're looking for.

After graduating from NC State, it's hard to believe I could have gone anywhere else. But I, along with a lot of other people, could be happy and have a wonderful college experience at a lot of different schools. As a public speaker, I travel from college to college all around the US. I've seen many schools that would have fit my criteria as a high school student that I could have been happy at.

The difference is college is what you make it. It's not about the color of the uniform or the record of the football team; it's what you do when you're at college that makes it a college experience.

When you hear of people having bad college experiences, it's usually because they choose to have that experience. They didn't take advantage of opportunities, or they let one stinky professor define their whole college career.

Don't be that person.

(If you *really* give it a shot and you're still finding yourself unhappy, then maybe talk to an advisor about your options or transferring).

Once you choose a school and step onto that campus, it's up to *you* to make the most of your four years (or five … or six).

Follow me and let's learn how you can make the most of it …

3 things you *want* in a school (example: a strong science program):

1)

2)

3)

3 things you *don't want* in a school (example: heavy commuter population):

1)

2)

3)

3 schools that fit these qualifications and their application deadlines:

1)

2)

3)

What I Learned As a First Generation College Student

Mari Ann Callais, Ph.D., Loyola University, New Orleans, Class of 1987

I was a first generation college student. For the first time in my life, my parents did not have the answers. They were as lost as I was. We did not understand financial assistance, so we all worked hard for me to go to college. It was truly a community effort. I lived in my uncle's home, my grandparents helped with monthly bills, my parents paid college tuition and transportation, and I worked a work study job and summers for all other financial needs. As a result, when I walked across the stage with my degree, it represented so many more people than just me.

If I could go back and do my college years all over again, I would do the following:

- *Major in something that I just loved instead of something I thought would be about a job. What you learn in college about yourself is just as important as the investment in the academic part of what you are learning.*

- *I would also take advantage of the resources available to me. I would find the most engaging faculty and just get to know them and them to know me. I did some of that, but I would be way more intentional than I was back then.*

- *I would study in another country. Studying abroad was not a big thing when I was in college, but if given the opportunity, I would do so this time around.*

Choosing a Major

Asking someone to write down on a piece of paper what they want to do for the rest of their lives is not an easy task, especially at 18 years old. Just like choosing a college, there's a lot of pressure on choosing the right major. Some people have known they wanted to be a teacher the first day of kindergarten. Some people know that math is their strong point and they want to work with numbers.

I was neither of those people.

I knew I liked to write. I guess I was kind of good at it. So, I thought, maybe I can be a writer for a magazine like *Cosmopolitan* or *Self?* And I could be one of those girls that walk around Manhattan in high heels sipping skinny mocha lattes like it's their job.

I wasn't that person either. I can't walk in heels.

However, I didn't know that from the start. Therefore, I chose a major with some wiggle room: communications. I'm not going to lie; I had to look up what communications actually meant on Wikipedia:

Communication studies *is an academic field that deals with processes of human communication, commonly defined as the sharing of symbols to create meaning. The discipline encompasses a range of topics, from face-to-face conversation to mass media outlets such as television broadcasting. Communication studies also examines how messages are* *interpreted through the political, cultural, economic, semiotic, hermeneutic, and social dimensions of their contexts.*

Whether or not you understand what that definition means (I certainly don't), I came to the conclusion that a lot of businesses need some kind of communications department. So my point is, choosing a major doesn't have to directly correlated to choosing your life's destiny. It's better to choose a major that can be applied to a lot of different careers than choose a more specific major like philosophy. If you're not exactly sure what you want to do, here are my do's and don'ts of choosing majors:

Go for it:

    Communications
    Business Administration
    Computer Science
    Psychology
    Finance

Unless you know this is what you want to do, really think twice about the following:

    Architecture
    Philosophy or Religious studies
    Anthropology
    Archeology
    Literature
    Art
    History

See my point? Choose a major with a lot of career opportunity, which is applicable to real life.

If you think you might want to go into history or something more specific, choose it as a minor. That way you're still being exposed to those classes without taking the big risk of having it as a major.

I saw too many of my friends make it to their junior or even senior year and realize that they had no idea what they were going to do with a history degree.

Keep your career options at a maximum.

My final piece of advice with choosing a major: think long-term and think broad. This may sound basic, but it's that simple: choose something that can bring you extensive career opportunities that will satisfy you.

Career Fields of Interest	Majors Relevant to Your Career		
	Major 1	Major 2	Major 3

Notes:

_____

_____

_____

_____

_____

_____

Style Tips: First Day Fool-Proof Outfit

Karly Hankin, Savannah College of Art & Design, 2012,
Founder of Peachy Keen Boutique

What to wear on your first day of anything can be exhausting. These days, work-dress is becoming more and more casual. Depending on where your first day is, here are some tips:

1. *A blazer is your best friend. Blazers can be dressed up or down, but always give off a professional vibe.*

2. *Something unique. Whether it's your pink shoes, chunky jewelry, headband, or what not, wear something they will remember you by.*

3. *Your attitude is the best accessory you have. Come in with ideas, positivity and eagerness. Believe it or not, this can make or break your outfit.*

First Day Of Class

First tip of advice: Don't be the girl that wears 4-inch heels and a low cut top. Almost every class has one. You'll attract attention, but not the right kind.

Second tip: Don't be the girl that wears the same pair of sweatpants for 5 days in a row. Especially with morning classes, it's easy to stay in "pajama mode" and just roll out of bed and walk to class. I remember thinking my reindeer pajamas would be "cute" to wear to my 8:00 a.m. class around the holidays. I was wrong.

It's fine every once in a while to dress down, but don't do it every day. You'll come across as sloppy and that cute guy that sits in front of you probably won't ask you to his formal that weekend … unless it's a pajama formal (which would be awesome).

A happy medium is jeans and a blouse. Maybe a cute pair of earrings or a necklace. Hair up or down with a little bit of makeup if you want to.

College isn't a runway show; but the way you dress is also a form of respect. Especially for your professor, it shows him or her that you're prepared and ready to take on the day.

Speaking of professors, don't be intimidated by the term "professor." If you're like me, I always associated professors with someone walking across the classroom slapping wrists with a ruler when someone couldn't recite Shakespeare perfectly.

Believe it or not, professors are human.

On my first day of COM 112, my professor came into the classroom in an octopus costume. Then she proceeded with a slideshow of all the favorite costumes she owned.

Random? Yes.

But I knew exactly what she was doing. She was humanizing herself to her students. The class was about 300 people. It can be very intimidating; it's difficult to gather the courage to talk to a professor that doesn't even know you're a student in his or her class.

Of course, most professors won't go to this extreme to make an intro to their students. It's up to you to make the first impression.

No matter the class size, it's easy to sit in the back and just float through the course just doing enough to get by. But that's not why you're paying tuition, is it?

Important tip: Before or after class on the first day, go up to the professor's desk and *shake his or her hand* and introduce yourself. You don't need to tell the professor your life's story or what you had for breakfast this morning. Just a simple, "Hi," (handshake) "my name is Jess. I just wanted to take a second to introduce myself. I'm really looking forward to your class this semester."

And that's it.

Whether or not he or she seems interested in your introduction, that prof will remember you in a good way.

Notes:

_____

_____

_____

_____

_____

_____

_____

_____

_____

_____

_____

_____

_____

_____

Where To Sit

Usually, where you sit on the first day is where you'll sit the rest of the semester. Either the teacher will make it your assigned seat or students will just naturally migrate to their usual seats.

Location, location, location.

Sitting in the back looks like you don't care. And, there are too many distractions for you to see when you should be staring at the board: computer screens, texting, a cute boy's head, etc.

It's not "nerdy" to sit in the front. There are fewer distractions, and you're more likely to be sitting beside other movers and shakers who will make super study buddies or group project partners. Plus, it shows the teacher you care.

Group Work

Some people love group work; some people hate it. No matter how much of a pain it is when someone isn't carrying his or her weight, this problem is never going to go away. There will always be circumstances in your life when someone doesn't pull through, so you're better off learning how to deal with it in college.

Here are some tips to get through group projects:

- **Don't team up with your best friends**: Partnering up with your friends for a grade has drama written all over it. If one of you isn't pulling his or her weight, it's going to put a strain on your relationship even when the project is over.

  Plus, hanging out and talking about unrelated topics will probably hinder your progress on the project. Keep your friends separate from your grades.

- **Establish goals**: As soon as your group is assigned, have a meeting with all of the group members. Decide how you're going to communicate. The most popular options are usually starting a group email or a Facebook group. Make sure everyone has each other's cell numbers, too.

Create a timeline for your project; break it down into separate goals and deadlines. This strategy will prevent procrastination and there should not be too much last minute work.

- **Give people roles**: During your initial meeting, discuss what the strengths and weaknesses are of the group members. If someone is better at design than he or she is at writing, have that person design the power point. If another member is good at researching but really bad at presenting, have that person take the lead in the research and give him or her a smaller role in the presentation.

Giving someone a specific role gives him or her more of a sense of responsibility. When you feel responsible for a part of the project, you're more likely to do it and do it well.

- **Practice, practice, practice**: Most group projects end with a presentation. Don't be that group that decides who's going to say what as they're loading their PowerPoint in front of the classroom. Meet the night before, or even a few times before that, and run through it at least three times.

Make it fun by splitting a pizza to ensure people will show up.

Try not to use flashcards. They can be distracting and you look more prepared if you talk from memory.

- **If someone is slacking:** I once had a group member whose name I didn't even know until the day of our presentation. Needless to say, I didn't put his name on the presentation. Don't be afraid to be the one to turn someone in. If someone in the group didn't do their part, start by confronting him or her. That's why you should always have emails and cell phone numbers for all team members.

"Hey (person's name), all of the members in the project group would really like to hit this project out of the park. I feel that you haven't been keeping up with (insert role here) like you were asked to do. If you don't have (insert task here) sent to me by Friday, I'm afraid I'll have to inform (insert professor name here). Thanks for understanding."

This doesn't mean you're mean or bossy. It means you can delegate, and you're not going to allow the professor to hand someone a good grade that doesn't deserve it. It's important to give honest reviews in group projects, which is why you shouldn't be in groups with friends. Usually teachers will have a peer review part at the end. Be honest with the review if someone didn't pull his or her weight even after you confronted him or her about it.

*Google Docs are great to use for group projects because everyone can edit them simultaneously without having to save and email to each other.

Presentations

I was one of those students that would rather do a presentation than take a test *any day*. I loved getting up in front of an audience and speaking, especially if I liked what I was talking about. One time I had to do a presentation about reproduction of insects and that was a different story.

However, not all people are eager to speak in public. In fact, most people dread public speaking, but you can't avoid it.

At some point in college, and probably in your career, you're going to have to stand up in front of people and give a presentation.

As a professional speaker, here are some tips I have for hitting it out of the park:

- **Know the guidelines:** Usually professors will give you a rubric of what's expected of you for the presentation. Make sure you know this inside and out. How long should it be? Can you use a Power Point? Is there a Power Point slide limit? Not knowing the requirements for the project is an easy way to lose points.

- **Go to the professor's office during office hours:** Ask your professor or teaching assistant if you can do a rehearsal of your presentation during his or her office hours. Getting feedback from the professor *before* you do it for a grade is a huge advantage and it shows the professor that you're serious about this project.

- **Rehearse on your own:** Do a dry run the night before. If there's a time limit or minimum, time yourself. Take into account if you speak faster when you're nervous. Reading it through in your head isn't enough. Say your presentation *out loud* so you can really understand where you need which parts you need to memorize better or what needs a better transition.

- **Dress appropriately:** Whether your teacher tells you to dress up or not, do it. Don't come in with gym clothes or jeans and sneakers. Dress the part. How you look is also a form of respect. Respect the assignment and dress professionally.

- **Don't read:** The most annoying habit is reading from a Power Point or flash cards during a presentation. I know it feels more comfortable to read text than to recite from memory, but it's your job to know the material. That's what a presentation is all about; it shows how well you know your topic. Turning your back and reading from the power point shows you're not prepared. Whatever visual source you're using should be for the benefit of the audience, not for you.

- **Slow down:** One of the most common nervous habits when speaking is speaking too fast. When practicing, make it a conscious effort to speak slowly. No one will be able to absorb your information if you're speaking a mile a minute. Remember, unlike you, your audience is hearing this material for the first time. What might seem like common knowledge to you is new to them. So take it slow.

- **Eye contact:** Circle the crowd with your eyes. Make eye contact with someone for 2-3 seconds then switch to another person. Don't just focus on the side of the room you're standing on; continuously switch your gaze to different parts of the room. Sometimes, students just look at the professor because that's who's grading them. But this presentation isn't just for them; it's for your classmates. Keep everyone engaged by bringing your focus to the whole room.

- **Strong conclusion**: What you don't want is that awkward clap because people don't know if the presentation is over or not. Have a clear ending and maybe even thank the audience for their time and welcome questions.

- **Encourage questions/discussion**: Questions are a great sign that people were engaged and interested in your presentation. Stay relaxed and don't ramble with your answers. Answer the question and then move to the next. If someone asks for your personal opinion on a topic like "Do you think it was fair that the media presented him in that light?" You can direct those kinds of questions to the audience and encourage a group discussion.

It's also important to note that it's okay to be nervous. People always ask me why I don't get nervous when I speak. I tell them I'm always nervous before a talk, I've just practiced not showing it. Nerves show that you care, which is a good thing. Instead of aiming to get rid of nerves before a presentation or a speech, learn to channel your nerves into energy and excitement for your talk.

When You Fail a Test or Assignment

It's most likely going to happen. I did it multiple times, and I survived. I found it usually happens at the beginning of the semester because you're not familiar with the professor's testing or grading styles.

The first time I did poorly on a test was in *Intro to Biology* my freshman year of high school. I remember looking at the grade and immediately breaking into a sweat. I felt embarrassed, dumb and unprepared for high school.

I thought about leaving with my head down and never coming back. I heard the teacher say before he dismissed the class, "If anyone has any questions or wants to go over their test, come see me after class."

I held my breath and walked up to his desk with my test in hand (now wrinkled and damp). I thought about coming up with a crazy story that prevented me from studying, something like my cat needed a haircut this weekend and I was the only one that could take him.

But here's the problem with that excuse ...

1. I'm not even a cat person
2. Do cats even get haircuts?
3. Even if they did, I doubt it would take more than a few hours
4. I'm a terrible liar

Once I quickly realized my cat story was a no-go, I said the only thing that came to my mind: "I don't understand the material."

The reaction I *thought* I'd get was rolled eyes and a response telling me I needed to study more to *learn* the material. However, Mr. Coggins said he'd be happy to meet with me after school and go over all the material from the test as well as what we would be learning the following week.

That same day, I stayed after school and we went over *everything*, one on one. Suddenly, photosynthesis and chlorophyll didn't seem like words in a foreign language anymore. Everything started to click.

When the next test came along, Mr. Coggins emailed me afterward and told me I received an A (and also the third highest grade in the class). From that point on, I learned that asking for help doesn't show weakness, it shows strength.

For my junior year of college history class, I had a teacher that was quite different from Mr. Coggins. On the first test, I studied for weeks for the test and I got an F. Not a C, not a D … a big fat red F (which was the perfect letter to describe my initial reaction).

It wasn't that I didn't know the material, I did. He counted all of my questions wrong because I didn't "elaborate" enough. I just answered the question and then moved to the next. This teacher wanted length. He would rather you write a good solid page about rainbows and butterflies than one or two sentences with the right answer. After I learned his ridiculous grading style, I got As on the rest of the tests in his class because I knew what he was looking for.

During my sophomore year of college, I took a philosophy class and we had the whole semester to write a huge paper. When I turned it in, I imagined I felt the same way Shakespeare did when he wrote his first play. Or maybe the way JK Rowling felt after she finished the first Harry Potter. It was *that* good (not to toot my own horn or anything).

When I got my final grade online, it said 85. An 85 is a B, which isn't bad, but my 20-pages of pure gold, which I had worked on for months, deserved at least a 90. My initial thought: *Would you have given Malcom Gladwell an 85 for writing Outliers?! No. And this is the same thing … basically.*

After about 5 minutes of yelling at my computer screen and doing a hand-stand against my wall to try to calm down, I decided I was going to approach my professor about this grade.

He said, "Actually, your paper was one of my favorites. It was such a shame you didn't provide a list of references at the end, or else you would have gotten a 95."

I flipped to the back of my paper to show him my *obvious* list of references.

He replied, "Oh, well, I guess that answers that. I must have missed it. I'll change the grade book now."

I replied, "Oh, okay, it's no big deal. Thanks."

Even though it was TOTALLY a big deal. But do you see what happened there? If I would have just continued to yell at my computer screen and do handstands, and if I had never talked to my professor, that grading mistake would have not been discovered.

Here are some tips on what to do if you didn't get the grade you wanted …

1) Don't freak out. Your dream job didn't just vanish in front of your eyes because of one bad grade. Take a deep breath and go to step number two.

2) Wait at least 3 hours before calling, emailing or approaching the professor. It's easy to say damaging things in the heat of the moment.

3) Ask your professor to meet *outside* of class to discuss your grade. Meeting during class will feel rushed and tense. Usually he or she will have office hours you can go to, but it's better to plant the seed in the professor's mind, so he or she can expect you.

4) Go over your assignment before you meet with the professor. Note where your weak points were, and come prepared with questions. If you feel like you have a question marked wrong that should have been considered right, come with support for your argument.

5) When you're meeting with your professor, ask as many questions as you can. This does two things:

   a. It shows your professor how dedicated you are as a student and how much you care about learning the material.

   b. It helps you learn his or her grading style. The more you know about what they want, the better you are on the next round.

*It's important to note that you need to keep your cool during a meeting with your professor, no matter how mad you are about your grade. Losing it on your professor will do nothing but lower their reputation of you. I know it's frustrating to get a lower grade than you think you deserve, but it's going to happen in life. If you handle it in a mature matter, they're more likely to see eye to eye with you.

Notes:

_____

_____

_____

_____

_____

Study Tips

Any time a professor offers a study session before an exam, go to it! Most likely, there will be little hints and tips about what's on the test. The professor usually wants to reward students who come outside of class to learn and prepare for an exam.

Although the library usually has a ton of resources, it also can be quite a social hub. If you're really looking for some uninterrupted studying, go to an empty classroom or a nearby coffee shop. You're less likely to get caught up in conversation with your friends like you might in the library.

I believe studying in groups is more effective than studying alone. When you study with a group, you have to plan ahead to get everyone together, so there is less likelihood that you'll procrastinate studying and leave it to the night before the test.

Another benefit of studying with a group is you can confirm any material that might be confusing to you or someone else in class. Material is better understood and retained when you have a group discussion. Students can also add new insight to a topic, which you might not have realized yet. Even if you know the material, explaining it to someone else also helps you remember it.

If you're in a big class and don't know enough people to form a study group, create a Facebook group with the title of the class, like HISTORY

206-SECTION 2. Find the roster if you have an online portal for the class (if not I'm sure the professor would give you the list) and invite classmates to join it. Then you can coordinate study groups on the page when it's time for a test.

However, be careful studying with friends. It's easy to go off topic from studying the Middle Ages to what you're going to wear to the formal the next weekend. Establish goals for each study session and make sure you reach them before you finish.

Tip: I use www.FlashcardMachine.com to make virtual flashcards. It's easier to study that way and you're not wasting paper for printing or money to buy flash cards. Plus, you can share them with your friends.

Electives

When picking classes, meet with your academic advisor first. An academic advisor's job is just what it sounds like: he or she advises you on which classes to take. Your advisor is extremely critical to your academic career. Advisors have the inside scoop on the classes you need and can line you up for success. If you feel your advisor isn't helpful, reach out to the department head and request a switch.

Get all of your requirements out of the way first. I've heard horror stories about students waiting until their senior year to take a required class and it was full so they couldn't graduate on time. Don't be that person.

But when you do have room for electives, pick them wisely. Don't just register for the classes that your friends will be taking. Pick classes that will benefit you. Here are some suggestions:

- **Photoshop**: Take any basic computer design class where you can learn Photoshop. Being able to put Photoshop skills on your resume makes you much more of a competitive applicant. The ability to design a basic flyer or Facebook timeline photo is 100 percent necessary in the professional world.
- **Foreign language**: I say go with Spanish, but conversational level of any foreign language is impressive and awesome for a resume. Businesses might do overseas work or want to grab a

larger market share at home. If you're bilingual, you can help with that.

- **Writing**: When I'm hiring, how a candidate writes is a huge deal to me. Even if I'm not hiring a person for a writing position, clear writing translates into clear thinking. If you can get your point across in a crisp and eloquent way, it will make you a more competitive candidate for a job, even just your writing in an email.

- **Financial planning**: No matter if you want to have a career with numbers or not, financial planning will help you with your career and in life. Learn how to make a spreadsheet and plan budgets. Knowing how to do both of these will look better on your resume for any job.

- **Public speaking**: No matter what job or field you go into, chances are you're going to have to present something to your peers or supervisors at some point. If you practice public speaking, you'll be better at getting your point across without feeling nervous. More importantly, being a confident public speaker gives you the opportunity to influence the world around you.

- **Internship**: Some schools offer internships for college credit. Some schools even require you to do an internship. Anytime you can get hands-on experience, even if it's not paid (which is a lot of internships), if you can afford to spend the time, take it.

Side note about registering for classes: Especially if you go to a big school, class registration can get super competitive. By the time it's your turn to register for classes, all of your top choices might be full. One of the benefits my school by being a campus tour guide was primary registration, which was a *huge* help. Talk to your advisor and see if there are any opportunities that allow you to register early.

Double side note about online classes: Nowadays, a lot of universities offer courses you can take online. I've done this a few times and have had mixed experiences. Keep in mind, there isn't a set time where you go to class and come home. It's your responsibility to make time for your online class and keep up with assignments. I recommend creating a calendar of all assignments due and tests as soon as you get the syllabus. Then, set a time each week to work on your online class, just like it's a regular class you have to attend.

Career fields that interest you.	Relevant Electives		
1.			
2.			
3.			

Notes:

_____

_____

_____

_____

_____

_____

_____

_____

Resources For You

Universities have a variety of specifically developed programs to make your college experience count. Some students don't even know they exist, so it's your job to find out what they are and take advantage of them.

Here are some resources you should look for ...

- **Career Center:** The career center is an extremely important place that often gets overlooked. It's filled with ways to not only figure out what you want to do after college, but how to do it.

    Usually the career center has databases full of career opportunities and career counselors to help you along the way. Meet with a counselor as soon as you start school so you can better plan out your college experience based on your career plans.

    Have the career center help you with creating a resume, cover letters and practice interviews. This is what they're here for, so don't miss out on it!

- **Technology Rentals:** Some schools have technology rentals in their library. For example, I was doing a project and needed to make a video, but didn't have a camera. I rented one from the library and rented the library software to edit the video.

You can also rent graphing calculators. Sometimes you can even rent computers.

- **Library:** At my school, our library has group study rooms, which are extremely useful for practicing group presentations without being interrupted.

  And, of course, libraries have books! Remember those paper things with all those pages? We're programmed to just Google anything these days, but sometimes using a good 'ole fashioned book is less distracting.

  Libraries also have librarians that can be extremely helpful. Some of them have certain backgrounds in different topics. Tell the librarian what kind of project you're working on and he or she can help you find the right resources.

- **Tutoring:** Originally, I had a bad taste in my mouth for the word "tutor." However, I learned that tutoring isn't just for people who are failing classes; it's for students who are maybe on that A/B border and want to bring it up to an A. A lot of schools have free tutoring centers or even Teaching Assistants (also called TAs) for certain classes that can offer help outside of class. Don't be afraid to get a little extra help here and there!

- **Fitness Center:** It's important to make time for exercise at college. You may have heard of a little thing called the "freshman fifteen" referring to first-year college students gaining weight due to all-you-can-eat dining halls, lack of sleep, alcohol consumption or stress. One step to avoid this phenomenon is utilizing your school's fitness center. Usually a gym is covered in your tuition, and sometimes they even have free fitness classes. Instead of going out to eat to socialize with your friends, go to a cardio dance class! Trust me, you'll feel awesome afterward.

- **Student Activities:** One of the best things about being in college is that there are departments designed to specifically enhance the lives of their students. The student activities department (or campus life, student affairs etc.) hosts a variety of programs to create a fun and educational environment for your college experience. When I was in school, I heard the founder of TOMS Shoes, a company that donates shoes to children in need, come speak at our campus. Hearing him speak sparked a fire in me to make a difference, which lead to me starting Headbands of Hope. Take advantage of campus activities … especially since they're usually covered in tuition!

Notes:

_____

_____

_____

_____

_____

_____

_____

_____

_____

_____

Speak Up!

Amanda Dinkel, North Carolina State University, Class of 2014

In high school, I was so afraid to speak in front of an audience that my teacher let me do presentations with my back to the class sitting down.

When I got to college, I knew I needed to start getting over my fear of public speaking, so I became a tour guide for prospective students and families visiting.

After shadowing a tour guide for the third time, I almost quit. No way was I going to be able to talk in front of groups of fifty or more people for an hour. But my friends and family encouraged me to just try it. So I did my first tour. And then I did another. And another.

By the time my senior year came around I felt more than comfortable speaking in front of crowds. I was signed up for extra tours. I sat on panels for the college in front of large admission of prospective students. My professors even asked me to speak to freshman classes of two hundred or more about college life, and to top it off … I spoke at my college graduation.

My advice to you is to use college to get over your fears. If public speaking scares you, involve yourself in areas where you're forced to do it. Trust me, you won't regret it!

Joining Clubs

College has tons of opportunities to join clubs and organizations that are not only socially beneficial, but also look great on your resume. Sure, join the Ping-Pong team for fun, but here are some clubs you consider should joining, which will help you prepare for your career ...

- **Become a tour guide:** I know you probably hated doing a lot of campus tours in high school.

   To your left is the first bathroom ever created on campus."

   But you probably didn't have the best tour guide if you were bored. Being a tour guide is a great way to gain public speaking experience. Sometimes I had groups as big as 200 people for a tour. The more you speak in front of people, the easier it gets. Therefore, when your new boss asks you to pitch a new idea to the whole office, you won't be as nervous.

   Tour guides also typically work with administration. One of the best letters of recommendation I ever received was from the administrator for the tour guides. Take every chance you get to network with the administration on campus.

Start as a freshman and give tours all four years. Campuses love hiring freshman to give tours because it adds diversity to their lineup, and they know they can have you on their team for more years. Don't worry if you don't know the history of the first dining hall or other random facts, they will teach you that.

- **Debate club:** Learn how to hold your own in a discussion. This skill is extremely helpful in business meetings and just in life in general. The debate club goes back to public speaking except it takes it to the next degree. Learn how to speak in a poised manner when you're under pressure and confrontation. This club is a no-brainer!

- **Student Government:** Not only will you be a voice on campus representing your student body, you'll learn how the school functions: what works and what doesn't work. Being in student government opens the door to gaining leadership skills on campus and working with the administration.

- **(Your major) Club:** If you're in pre-med, join the pre-med club. If you're in media, join the student media team on campus. You'll not only meet people that are probably in your classes, you'll have the opportunity to network with people in your field. And, of course, you can gain a group of study buddies who are probably in your same classes.

- **Philanthropy Club:** Joining a club that does work for charity or volunteering in the community will help you gain a better perspective while you're in college. Plan a canned food drive or get a group together and clean up your local park. Bring board games to a senior citizen home or visit your local children's hospital. There are so many ways you can get a group together on campus to give back to your local community. Of course this looks great on a resume, but do it for the bigger purpose and change lives.

- **Start one!** If you've always wanted to have a book club on campus but there isn't one, start it! Or if you want to get a group of people together to run every Monday and Wednesday evening, start it. No matter what the club or organization is, it says a lot about your drive, organizational skills and work ethic if you build something from the ground up.

When picking a club or activity, it's important to look for three things:

1) Will it provide you with any public speaking opportunities?
    a. Whether or not you like standing up and speaking in front of a crowd, it's always good to practice in college. Like I said, I was a tour guide and a fitness instructor. It was intimidating at first, but I got so used to public speaking that it didn't seem scary anymore.
2) Will you be able to plan an event from start to finish?
    a. Heading up an event says a lot about you. It says you can delegate, you can be creative, and you can work hard. Volunteer to head up planning an annual event for your club.
3) Will this club provide you networking opportunities with administration?
    a. Getting to know your professors in class is great, but the supervisors or administrators for your club get to know you on another level. When it's time to start applying for jobs or even scholarships, you'll need letters of recommendation and references. Try to pick a club where you can work closely with members of the administration so you can later ask them for references.

Try to join a couple of these kinds of clubs your freshman or sophomore year so you can stick with them throughout your college experience. It looks better to have committed to one or two clubs for four years than bouncing around to a lot of different clubs throughout college. And don't forget to throw in some fun and random clubs, like ballroom dancing or arts and crafts!

	Clubs You Want to Join		
	Club 1	Club 2	Club 3
Contact Information			
Meeting Times			

Notes:

_____

_____

_____

_____

_____

_____

_____

_____

_____

_____

_____

PART 2: SOCIAL

Being Healthy On the Inside and Out

Amber Krsys, Point Park University, Class of 1998,
Founder of bodyheart.com

"Beauty is an inside game. The only way to win is to start from within."
~ Amber Krsys, founder of bodyheart.com

College is a time for forming new ideas of yourself—who you are and how you relate to the world. One incredibly important relationship that is often disregarded is your relationship with your body. Basically, how you feel in your own skin.

It's easy to fall victim to societal pressure and assume your worth and value are based in your appearance. That your body is flawed in some way and needs to be 'fixed' in order to feel more confident, happy and have the life you want to live.

*This is one of the biggest illusions in existence. Your worth and value are innate within YOU. And, your body can be a powerful asset in experiencing this if you choose it to be. One way you can do that is by getting curious about your body. What does your body like to eat? (**Not you, your body!**) What foods make her thrive? What exercises? How does she feel most often? How do you want to feel most often?*

Learning to listen to your unique body is the key. Doing that can save your life—literally! It certainly saved mine.

Slowing down and starting from within is the best way to embrace all that makes you special. Being you—authentically you—is truly the antidote to guilt, shame and not-enoughness. After that, practice kindness and compassion for yourself. And, lastly, don't be afraid to seek support. The resources available to you on your campus are there for a reason. In fact, many of those resources will not be available to the same extent when you graduate, so use them now.

You only get one body in this life. She is yours. Claim her. Celebrate her and see what unfolds from there.

Staying Healthy

Don't be intimidated by "The Freshman Fifteen." It's this huge phenomenon that college makes you fat. There's not some crazy weight-gain curse that's bestowed upon you on your first day of class. The phenomenon comes from the increase of choices you have. In college, there are more choices for everything: what classes to take, who you want to be friends with, and what you want to eat. There are a lot of choices that might not be the healthiest: dorm room vending machines, dining halls, and 2 a.m. deliveries.

On the other hand, there are also plenty of choices to allow you to stay healthy and fit.

I came from a family of health nuts. My parents took pride in preparing well-balanced meals for my sister and me. Consequently, I never really cooked for myself.

Also, I was a year-round athlete in high school. I always had practice after school, so I never needed to worry about working out on my own. So college was a change for me, health-wise. Healthy meals weren't just handed to me and workouts weren't preplanned. But just like academically, college has a variety of resources to help stay healthy around campus.

Campus Health Tips:

Look up dining hall menu:
Usually, dining halls have nutrition information available online.
If you look up the menu beforehand, you can plan out a healthier
meal and avoid dishes with hidden calories.

Keep healthy snacks in your dorm room:
Don't wait for the three main meals. It's better for your metabo-
lism if you eat healthy snacks throughout the day like almonds or
carrots. If you have chips and candy in your room, you'll be more
likely to choose those over your healthier options.

Always eat breakfast:
Start your day off right with a good meal when you get up.
Whether you're rolling out of bed at noon or up at the crack of
dawn for class, make sure you start your day with a balanced,
healthy meal.

Leave early to walk, no bus:
Larger campuses usually have a bus or some kind of public transportation system for students. Instead of taking the bus everyday,
get some extra exercise by leaving early and walking to class.

Stair challenge:
When I was in college, my friends and I would team up and do
the "stair challenge" every few weeks. No elevators or escalators,
only stairs. So if you lived on the nineteenth floor of the dorm,
you really felt the burn.

Go to group fitness classes:
Instead of going out to dinner or froyo with your friends to socialize, take advantage of the free fitness classes your school
might have to offer. Go to an evening yoga class or team up with
a friend and go to boot camp on Monday and Wednesday morn-
ings. If your school doesn't have fitness classes, look up workouts
on Pinterest with your friends and then do them at the gym.

Take a PE class every semester:
If it's harder for you to schedule going to the gym, make it a requirement by taking a PE class. Typically PE classes are 2-3 days per week. Not only are you getting a consistent workout, you can learn new ways to stay healthy. One semester I took a rock climbing class, and I worked muscles I didn't even know I had. Since you're already paying for these through your tuition you may as well take advantage and get a workout that will help keep you in shape and motivate you.

Sleep
Lack of sleep not only makes you cranky, it makes you crave sugar. Try to develop a sleeping routine instead of random hours. Sleeping similarly every night helps with falling asleep easily. Also, leave your bed for sleeping. Any studying, eating or watching Netflix should be done at your desk or on your couch. Only sleeping in your bed helps trigger your mind to go to sleep when you crawl in.

Notes:

_____

_____

_____

_____

_____

_____

_____

Don't Break Your Wallet

Let's face it: If you're a college student, you probably don't have the savings yet to buy that yacht you've always wanted. Part of the fun of being in college is being broke. I know that sounds strange, but living frugally can be seen in two ways: a downside or an adventure.

I picked adventure.

It's easy to blow money on eating out with friends or shopping for new game-day outfits for the football game on Saturday. But you can still have fun without breaking the bank.

Here are some tips for saving money:

Get used books on Amazon:
Textbooks add up ... big time. Don't wait until one month into class to buy your book because all of the used copies might be sold out (plus you'll be behind on reading). Get your book list early and find deals on Amazon to save a few bucks. When the semester is over, you can sell them back on Amazon, as well.

Become a Resident Advisor:
A lot of schools have opportunities to be a resident advisor (RA) at a dormitory. You're responsible for the well-being of the stu-

dents in your hall or unit. Usually, you get free rent and your own room. Need I say more?

Find a discount theater:
Sometimes college campuses have student theaters that are free or really cheap! Don't waste money on regular theaters (tickets can be crazy expensive). Find an inexpensive theater or wait until it comes out on DVD.

Use your meal plan:
This sounds like a no-brainer, but if you have a meal plan, use it! I know it's tempting to go to that new Asian restaurant down the street, but you didn't prepay for lo mein. If you prepay for food, don't let it go to waste. Sometimes dining halls let you get food to-go. If so, take advantage of that. Pick up peanut butter packets and fruit to snack on for later. If they have oatmeal packets, you've hit the jackpot.

Buy a water bottle:
Don't waste your money on bottled water. Get a cool, hip water bottle and refill it regularly. Maybe even put a sweet bumper sticker on it?

Student discounts:
A lot of businesses (big and small) offer student discounts. For example, Apple offers student discounts. Some airlines and travel agencies do, as well. Same with movie theaters (if you *must* see the film in theaters). Always ask if there is a student discount available.

Pick up your local paper:
Read your local town paper and school paper for freebies and festivals coming up. Maybe you'll get lucky and find an event with free food.

Share clothes:

Find friends that share your same passion for fashion and share clothes to kill that shopping urge.

Resale stores:

If you must shop, start at consignment stores. *Plato's Closet* is one of my personal favorites. Bring clothes that you don't wear anymore and sell them. Either take the cash, or you can use it as credit and swap for clothes at the store (they give you a higher value if you swap).

Live near campus:

When you can walk to campus, you'll save a ton of money on parking (my school was $350 per semester) and save money by not using public transportation. Plus, it's super convenient to live close by.

Apply for scholarships:

Always keep tabs on scholarships. There are *millions* of them. This is a great way to get funds towards tuition or even just to pay for your books.

Sell your expertise:

Get a job on campus or create one yourself. If you're really good at math, start a small tutoring business. If you're good with technology, troubleshoot computer issues in exchange for a few bucks. Offer a résumé writing service if you're good at it. Find what you're good at and try to make a few extra bucks doing it.

Making Friends

Emily Wheet, North Carolina State University, Class of 2014

During my first week of college, I was trying to make friends with anyone and everyone. I had a few people that I would hang out with regularly, however I was only friendly with them because they lived on my hall in my dorm. I knew we did not have much in common, but I didn't want to eat breakfast, lunch, and dinner alone in the dining hall. I was starting to get worried that being in such a new and big environment, I wouldn't find a true friend. But one day, when I least expected it, that changed.

It all started with a game called Apples to Apples. *Picture twelve freshmen on day five of living the college life. We felt invincible. We were packed into a dorm room not much bigger than a closet, but it felt perfect because there were no adults telling us to make our beds.*

One guy in the room kept picking my card (coincidentally). From then on, this guy and I have been best friends for the past five years. **Everyone** *has always thought there was a love interest. But I want to tell you that it's okay to be best friends with a guy. It is actually pretty awesome!*

But besides that, put yourself out there when you get to college and do things you love or that you think are fun (like Apples to Apples). *Because when you involve yourself in things you like, you're going to meet like-minded people.*

Finding Friends

To rush or not? I thought about joining a sorority a lot during my college career. I think your decision to rush your freshman year depends a lot on your family (if you come from a family of "Greeks") or if the people you already know (like your roommate or suitemates) are all rushing. Or, it's just something that always interested you.

For me, I became involved with the fitness team on campus early my freshman year so that became my "sorority." I made friends with like-minded people and we all threw events together. I started my company and then that consumed a lot of my time. Therefore, I didn't see the need to rush and join a sorority.

However, I think any way you can involve yourself with a group of people is important in college. Whether it's Greek life, debate club, student government, tennis club or anything else where you can join a group of people with similar interests, it is crucial to your college experience.

When you're in a group setting you create that familiarity, which can make a large college campus seem smaller, and sometimes you need that.

Greek life has a lot of advantages: a ready-made social life, philanthropic involvement, academic boosts with your sisters, a limitless wardrobe and leadership opportunities. However, be cautious that you don't shut yourself off to non-Greek communities.

No matter what "group" you're in, just remember to be open-minded and keep your social scene diverse.

Which brings me to diversity …

I feel like this word carries two different meanings for me from high school to college.

In high school (I went to a super small high school), I felt like I was "stuck" in the same group of people, and it just didn't feel quite right. The things the group members valued, I didn't feel the same way. I didn't really care what kind of car a boy drove (or if he even had a car). I didn't care if people saw me without makeup. And I didn't care if my purse was a *Coach* purse or one from a thrift shop.

But I thought if I tried to get to know other people, I'd be resented for reaching outside "the group." And high school friend groups can be like that sometimes. Once you're in, you're in. And there's no wandering elsewhere.

Even though that's entirely false because it's a free country, I didn't feel that way. It was only when I did sports, where I was able to branch out and meet new people that things began to change. This is one of the things I loved about being on a team.

I purposefully went to a college that very few people from my high school attended. My first thought at freshman orientation was, "I better pick my new group wisely because I'll be with them for four years." I couldn't have been more wrong. I barely remember the names of the people in my orientation group with the exception of one or two. In college, you're not confined to lunch tables and locker talk. You're able to float freely from person to person without having to "dub" yourself into a certain group.

Diversity gained a whole new meaning when I got to college. It was so refreshing to be friends with so many different people of different backgrounds and interests. Sure, I could have done the same in high school. But

I was too caught up in my own world of "groups." In college I learned to appreciate the differences in people and learned from them.

By the time I graduated, I found three people who I knew I'd be in touch with forever. But I had hundreds of other friends who I never would have found if I wasn't open to change.

Notes:

_____

_____

_____

_____

_____

_____

_____

_____

_____

_____

_____

_____

_____

Social Media

By the time I finish writing this chapter, I will probably have checked my Facebook three times ... or five. That's our reality. As millennials, we accept that our world of communication is changing. While other generations are complaining about out it, we're embracing it. If we're at a red light, chances are we're going to take those 10 seconds to tweet, check our Facebook or see if we got any likes on Instagram (then put our phone away before we drive).

Some say we're addicted; I say we're adaptive.

I would argue that our generation was quicker to understand that our world just became smaller. We're not limited to what we can see and share from our front door; we now have the capacity to reach much further.

When I started to build my audience with Headbands of Hope, I knew I wanted to appeal to 20-something females because I knew they wouldn't just buy my product, they'd blast it through all their social media outlets, too. So technically, we control what's popular because we have the ability to make something important go viral with a few clicks, like twerking.

Okay- maybe not all *important* things but you get the point.

Contrary to the millennial stereotype, we haven't lost the ability to communicate face-to-face. We will still meet up for a cup of coffee for human interaction ... but we're going to take a selfie while we're there.

Here are some apps that I love (that are free):

HelloSign:

I can't stand printing out papers to sign and rescan. I'd like to say I hate doing this because it's a waste of paper (which is true), but honestly, it just takes too much time for a simple signature and send. HelloSign makes it simple to sign papers virtually. Just scan your signature one time and then upload it to a document whenever you need it. Super simple.

Hipmunk:

Hipmunk makes booking travel plans easy. With my speaking travel schedule, I need an app that makes booking flights simple. With Hipmunk, you can filter flights by price or even agony. But my favorite thing about it is you can email a booking to your computer, so you can book from there. And, of course, you can sign up for fare alerts, which is always helpful!

Postagram:

Want to send a thank you card to someone? Or a birthday card? Make it personalized by uploading a picture of you and that person to this app and send the postcard from your phone and it will show up in their mailbox in days (0.99 for each card).

Square:

If you're selling a product, you know how hard it is to handle cash. Plus, a lot of people don't even carry cash anymore. Square lets you accept credit cards through the swipe of your phone. Of course, there is a transaction fee, but it's worth it with the additional business you bring in by accepting cards.

Tripit:

With my company and public speaking, I'm on the road a lot. Tripit puts all of your travel plans into one itinerary. All you have to do is forward your travel confirmations to them!

PicLab:

If you're an Instagrammer, this app takes filter and editing to the next level. Add text and design to your photo straight through your phone. Then upload it to Instagram or just save it to your library with one click.

Podcasts:

Since I'm on the road a lot, sometimes music won't cut it. I need to hear stories or feel intellectually stimulated. Downloading the podcast app allows you to categorize your podcasts and download new ones. Some of my favorite podcasts are TED Radio Hour and Radiolab.

Map My Run:

When I'm in a new town or city, I don't have time to plan out where the sidewalks are or map out a route. Map My Run uses your location and looks up previously mapped runs in that area. You can also log your own runs with this app. The most helpful feature is that it tells you your split time through your music every mile.

Tabata Timer:

This app creates a beeping 20-second interval timer through your phone. If you want to be timed doing 8 20-second sets of crunches, it's easier to use this app instead of looking at a timer because it beeps through your music.

Starbucks:

Let's face it, who can do all the above without coffee?

Roommates

If living with a random stranger in a cellblock room smaller than my closet doesn't sound like fun, I don't know what does.

Okay, maybe I'm being a little sarcastic. But seriously, it's not that bad. It's a part of the college experience.

When picking a roommate, I think it's better to go with someone you don't know. Let's say you move in with your best friend, or even just someone you know from high school, I guarantee you two will be glued at the hip during all the welcome week activities, and you're going to have a tough time putting yourself out there and meeting new people.

One of the biggest misconceptions about roommates is that they need to be your best friends and you need to do *everything* together. Well, I'm here to tell you that's not true. One of the best roommates I ever had was an exchange student from Paris, and she taught me how to make crepes. Need I say more?

We didn't hang out really, but we were both respectful of each other's space. We didn't blast music or talk on the phone late at night. We didn't eat each other's food. We just coexisted … and it was awesome.

But out of the four years you have roommates, there's going to be a bad apple in there. If you had no roommate problems at all your whole college career, you were probably the problem.

Here are some common issues and how to tackle them:

She talks with her boyfriend late at night during the week.

Super annoying. Especially when you have a test the next day. Here's a way to tackle it:

"I know it must be super hard having a boyfriend at a different school, but after 10:00 pm I'm trying to go to sleep for my classes the next day. Would it be okay if you took the conversation outside if it's after 9:30?"

She eats your food.

If there's one thing I love, it's food. And if someone is eating my cereal, I will go karate kid on them.

Instead of doing that, here's a way to tackle it:

"I know Cheerios are SUPER addicting! Would you mind picking up the next box since we shared this one?"

She's a mess. I can't see the floor!

This one's a little more awkward, but you have to say something.

"College is so crazy with all of these tests and papers! With so much time being busy, it's hard to keep the room in line, but the clutter is becoming distracting. If you could pick up your stuff off the floor, I'll do a vacuum after."

You'll probably run into more, but just be respectful and confront your roommate *lightly*. The easiest way to start an argument is to come into it full force like "STOP EATING MY CHEERIOS!" Even though that's what's going through your head, approach the situation softly. If it doesn't change, then maybe you should consider using a little more force.

One of the perks to having a bad roommate is you become more active and involved because you don't want to go back to your dorm. I know it sounds silly, but when I had a bad roommate I did everything I could to avoid going home: I played intramural racquetball, I studied in the library, I went to the farmers market, and I volunteered on the weekends. I even joined a snowboarding club and went on trips with them. I slid down the mountain on my butt the whole way … but at least my roommate wasn't there! See my point?

Tip: If you ever feel unsafe or threatened by your roommate, always contact the Resident Director in your building.

Studying Abroad

Kate Thomas, University of Southern California, Class of 2006,
Founder of TravelwithKate.com

It was the summer before my senior year of college. With one short year left, I was almost finished and ready to head out into the "real" world. But I had one big regret. I hadn't experienced a semester abroad. And despite having fantasized about taking one in Paris, I never put the wheels in motion to make it happen. Sadly, it seemed it was too late now.

Less than a month before school would begin in September, I started reading online about my school's study abroad programs. I was surprised to find out that if I could just take a language placement exam in three weeks time and score into level II French, I would be eligible to go to Paris for my final semester of college. The only problem? I'd never taken a French class in my life!

I took it as a challenge and signed up for an immersion class at a local language school. For four hours a day for three weeks I studied vigorously with my instructor (a burp-ey, old, Parisian man named Pierre). Some days he would sit in the classroom at the language school drilling me on verb tenses and sentence structure. Other days we would sit in a nearby café and use stories about his former life in Paris for vocabulary lessons. Amazingly, I felt myself getting a grip on the basics of the language during our time together. It also helped that I studied for hours on my own after each class.

And then came test day. After only three short weeks, I found myself in a big, stadium-like lecture hall taking a French placement exam. I knew I had a strong base, but when the oral section began and the snobby-sounding lady over the loud speaker started testing us with phrases and words that sounded diabolically similar to each other, I was sure I'd fail. Ils ont. Ils sont. If you know any French, you know how hard these are to distinguish from each other for a beginner.

The next four days of waiting for my results were totally nerve wracking. I began to formulate backup plans. "I could go to Spain or Mexico," I thought. I had already taken Spanish II at school. But luckily, I didn't have to change course. On that fourth day, I looked online and found that I had placed into French II. It felt like a miracle! I was eligible to study abroad in Paris. Now, I had only to apply for the program!

Ultimately, I did go to Paris. I studied art history taking field trips to the Louvre and Musee D'Orsay each week to view the original, classic works of art. I took a French class at the famed Sorbonne University and visited the EU headquarters in Brussels with my International Relations class. I made friendships with classmates in my program and local Parisians, which will last a lifetime. And during my six months in Paris, I had experiences that planted the seeds that would later lead me to choose my career path.

Without my time in France, my life would be completely different and I fear much less aligned with my true calling in life. Don't make the mistake I did, jeopardizing my chances to go to my top study abroad destination. Be sure to prioritize study abroad during your college experience because there is nothing more enriching than travel!

Studying Abroad

I minored in Spanish with the dream of studying abroad in Spain … and ordering my meals in Spanish at Mexican restaurants to impress my friends.

However, the summer before my trip was when I interned for Make-A-Wish and got the idea for Headbands of Hope. I knew if I went abroad and came back in six months and tried to create Headbands of Hope, I wouldn't have the same passion and eagerness to work as I did then.

So I cancelled my trip, built my company and never looked back.

To me, starting my business was my college adventure. Now that I'm self-employed, I have the flexibility to travel when I want.

However, my story is different than most.

College is the perfect time to travel and see parts of the world you want to see. To be able to get an education and immerse yourself in a different culture at the same time is an amazing experience. When you graduate, you'll most likely get a job or go to grad school immediately following. Then after you get a job you might meet the man of your dreams and get married and have kids.

My point is there will always be excuses not to just pack up and go explore the world. But there will not always be opportunities that support you in doing this.

Study abroad programs in college are built to support your desire to travel and learn. There are so many programs that are only available to you as a student. Consult your study abroad department at your school for opportunities.

Programs that you to take to that country	Countries You Want to Visit		
	Country 1	Country 2	Country 3
Program 1:			
Program 2:			
Program 3:			

Notes:

_____

_____

_____

_____

_____

_____

_____

_____

Spring Break

Some of my greatest college memories came from spring break. Sure, I had fun on a cruise with my friends one year, but my favorite spring break was through a program my school offered called Alternative Spring Break. Students chose a service project in a part of the world and worked there for a week.

I chose working at a school with underprivileged children in New Mexico. I had my own first grade classroom and worked with the kids on reading, writing, math, telling time and so much more. I quickly realized that they weren't used to getting this much attention and care.

Even though I wasn't lying on a beach drinking out of a pineapple, that spring break was my favorite.

Find out through your student activities department if there are any spring break opportunities you can be involved in on campus. Even if it's not a service project, sometimes schools have guided trips like kayaking or rock climbing with a group of students. These trips are a great way for you to meet new people and they're typically more affordable than your average trip.

Notes:

Overcoming Shyness

Tammy Tibbets, The College of New Jersey, 2007, Founder of ShesTheFirst.org.

When I was a senior in high school, I was voted Most Shy in the yearbook—that was such a wakeup call for me. I didn't want to go through life known as the girl who didn't speak up! I had a voice to use as I wished—in a world where far too many women were violently silenced, in a country where so many women fought hard for my generation to have that freedom—and I wasn't using it. I was standing in my own way. So, when I went to college I majored in journalism. At that point, I wasn't quite sure what my own message to the world was, but I knew I was good at listening and writing. I resolved to use my voice to amplify the voices of other women who were doing inspiring things to make the world better.

One challenge I gave myself was to run for a student government office. The first thing I did after moving into the dorms was join the student council elections, hoping to be secretary. I wrote and delivered a speech, dressed in professional black pants and a sweater—truly making myself dive head first into the waters of public speaking. I lost the election to a young woman who dressed far less professionally in a short denim skirt and white tank top and stuck Post-Its all over her body during her speech to illustrate her point. If I sound bitter, well, I was at the time; but now it's just funny to me. It all worked out for the best. As a journalism student, I was better positioned to sit in student government meetings as a reporter. The real point is I won the challenge I gave myself. I proved I wasn't going to be known as the Most Shy ever again.

Fast forward to senior year when I was selling some books back to the bookstore. The cashier was a member of my graduating class and said, "I remember you! I voted for you to be class secretary freshman year. That was a great speech." I don't know how she remembered that, but it meant a lot to me.

Parties

All right, listen up. I'm going to tell you something that took me a long time to realize, and it will change your whole college experience. So listen closely ...

People don't care if you drink or not.

I thought college was one big mosh pit of peer pressure to take shots and do keg stands. But I learned that it really doesn't matter if your cup filled with sprite has vodka in it or not. People always talk about the girl that got so drunk she danced on the table or the guy that was so wasted he put his mattress on the roof. But being the topic of conversation doesn't make you "cool." In fact, it makes you predictable and uninteresting.

These are reasons why you shouldn't be "the drunk girl" ...

1) **Pictures last forever**
   When you're drunk, you might not realize or even care if people are taking pictures of you. But those pictures can do major damage. If there is a picture on Facebook of you doing a keg stand or passed out on the couch, you can forget about getting that job you wanted.

2) **Sober people think you're stupid**
   When you drink, alcohol makes you feel confident and

cool. Therefore you do things you might not normally do in your right state of mind. When you're in a group of people slurring your words and rambling on and on about the last Kardashian episode, you're not creating the best image for yourself.

3) You pass out

No one wants to be a canvas for sharpies when they're passed out on the couch. Not to mention, it's dangerous physically and you can get your belongings stolen.

4) Drunk actions are real

You can't take back what you said or did when you were drunk. The response "but I was drunk" doesn't negate making out with your best friend's boyfriend or dialing your ex 100 times. Those are just minor things compared to what could happen: You could have unprotected sex, lose your virginity to a stranger or get in the car with a drunk driver. You can't take back what happened when you were drunk.

5) It's illegal

If you're under 21, don't drink. You'll see people drinking underage, but it doesn't mean it's okay. Not only do the reasons above apply to you, it's worse. If you get caught (which is likely), it's on your record and it's a lot of money for court fees. When you're applying for a job and they see you got caught underage drinking, your chances of getting hired drop dramatically.

But being realistic, waiting until you're legal can be hard. I suggest making a "deal" with yourself or even with your parents. The deal could be if you make it to 21 without drinking, you get to go on that trip you've always wanted or you buy yourself an iPad. It sounds silly, but when you have something else on the line as motivation it can make you stay strong in high-pressure situations.

However, being drunk is not the same as having a few drinks. *When you're legal*, it's okay to have a few drinks with your friends or go to a party.

Here are my tips on how to stay safe when drinking …

1) **Drink water**
   It's really important to stay hydrated with water when drinking alcohol. Alcohol makes you dehydrated, and that dehydration causes hangovers. When you go to sleep that night, keep a pitcher of water by your bed.

2) **Eat first**
   Eating before you drink will help the alcohol to absorb slowly. If you're drinking on an empty stomach, you can get drunk way too fast and pass out. Make sure you eat a balanced meal before you drink.

3) **Plan your transportation**
   The last thing you want to do is get stranded when you're drinking. Call a cab or arrange transportation beforehand. If there are a lot of people going to and from downtown, arrange a party bus. If you do get a ride with someone, make sure that person hasn't been drinking at all beforehand.

4) **Use the buddy system**
   I know this sounds like kindergarten, but always have a buddy. Having someone with you at all times helps in keeping each other safe. If someone loses their wallet and can't get a cab ride home, it's important to have a buddy with you for that. If a guy is being too forward with you at a bar, your buddy can step in and be there for you.

5) **Don't accept drinks you didn't see poured**
   If a guy comes up to you and offers you a cranberry vodka he has in his hand, don't take it. You don't know what's in that drink because you didn't see it being poured. You don't want to risk drinking something that could have drugs in it. If

you're hitting it off with a guy and he offers to buy you a drink, go with him to the bar and watch it get poured and handed to you.

6) **No shots**

Shots are super dangerous. You could be feeling completely sober, and then have a shot or two and be completely drunk. Tossing back straight alcohol is never a good idea. If it's a big group of people and they're all passing out shots, either say no or fake it. Most likely you all take the shot at the same time, so when everyone tosses their head back and takes the shot, just toss yours on the ground. No one will know the difference!

Going out with your friends is fun and exciting; just make sure you're doing it safely. Remember to keep it classy (and fabulous)!

Notes:

_____

_____

_____

_____

_____

_____

_____

Safety On Campus

Take out your phone right now ... have it yet? Okay, now look up the number for your campus police and SAVE IT INTO YOUR PHONE.

Sorry for yelling (even though you can't hear me). But this is just super important. When you're on campus you have specific campus police there to help you. It's much more efficient to go through them if there is an issue rather than dialing 9-1-1.

Here are some tips on how to stay safe on campus:

- Don't walk alone, especially at night. I know we just talked about using the buddy system when drinking, but also do it when you're sober. Walking home from the library when it's dark can be very dangerous. If you don't have anyone to walk home with, your campus police should have an escort system. Don't be embarrassed to use it! It shows that you're smart and prepared.
- Don't post on social media that you're "home alone." This is a total no-no that we don't think about a lot. Also, be sure you're not using location services about where you live.
- Don't let anyone into your dorm or apartment building you don't know. Your dorm building should be locked. Sometimes, people are waiting for a friend outside the dorm to let them in and might ask you to just let them in instead.

Don't do it. Who cares what they think. You don't know who they are or what their intentions are going into a dorm building they don't live in.

- Make sure someone knows where you are at all times. This sounds silly, but it's important. Going to the mall? Spending the night at a friend's place? Going on a date? Let someone know. That way if anything happens, someone knows where you're supposed to be.

I might sound like I'm being overly cautious and that's fine. In this day and age, I'd rather be overly cautious than unprepared. Don't wait until there's a problem to learn about safety on your campus and what they have to offer.

To Go the "Distance" or Not?

Lauren Athey, Eastern Carolina University, Class of 2014

In my opinion, it's not a good idea to do the long distance relationship with your high school sweetheart. You go to college to find the individual you want to be, do that and do that on your own. You will not be the same person four years later and neither will he.

Trust me, it's from experience. My high school sweetheart and I decided to try and make it work, going to college less than two hours apart. Within the first semester, I saw the true colors of our relationship.

I was so determined to make it work, I put in for a transfer to his university after my freshman year. I should have noticed the red flag waving when he did not jump for joy when he found out about my acceptance to his college. But I guess you could say I was "blinded by love."

I never gave my first college a chance. I never branched out to meet new people and join fun clubs. I was so caught up in the life my high school sweetheart and I once had, instead of being caught up in my own life and studies. Needless to say, it didn't end well, but I learned a lot about myself.

Go to college to find YOU. There are plenty of fish in the sea (and really cute fish actually). These next four years, you're allowed to be selfish. Love yourself first. Focus on your life and your goals. You don't need anyone else to justify that.

Dating

Your first day of college will be overwhelming with the people you meet (and people that catch your eye). It's a fresh playing field and new arena of possibilities. That guy that held the elevator for you in your dorm could be your future boyfriend ... or even husband. Let's not get ahead of ourselves ...

There are so many opinions on college relationships and if they're even worth your time. You hear so many rules about relationship boundaries, when to date or when not to date.

Let's try to simplify it by defining what I believe is now the dating vocabulary.

Talking: You've maybe gone out once, you text during the day, but you're not exclusive yet.

Hooking up: You have sexual relations, but you're not going out on dates or calling each other to talk. Basically, you're friends with benefits (which can be extremely complicated).

Dating: You've both decided to be with each other exclusively.

Seems pretty simple. Right?

Wrong.

Why do you think there are so many reality shows, songs, movies, poems and other literature about love? Because it fascinates everyone with its complexity. There are so many different stages, opportunities, and life-changing moments that come with relationships.

Every person has a need for human touch and connection. Meaning, love is universal, no matter what language you speak. So when people say you shouldn't date in college or you shouldn't trust men, they're just holding people back from our natural desire to find a connection with someone else.

Most likely, the first person you date won't be the person you marry. But that's what dating is for: finding out what you want and don't want in a significant other.

So the rules to dating in college are simple: There are none.

People will tell you to be single and go crazy, or people will tell you you're going to meet your future husband. But the great part is this isn't about people telling you what you want, it's about you finding out what you want. Forget all the articles you've been reading about how dating should or shouldn't be, and focus on what you want yourself.

After all, dating is about being happy with someone else, and the only person that can determine that is you.

Tip: If you feel that you're ready to be sexually active, go to your student health center and ask any questions you have and what protection they can provide you. Don't be embarrassed; they'll be happy that you're being smart and thinking ahead.

Notes:

_____

_____

_____

_____

_____

_____

_____

_____

_____

_____

_____

_____

_____

_____

_____

What "I Don't Want Anything Serious" Actually Means ...

Picture this: The guy that's been flirting with you all semester finally asks you out. You go to dinner, hang out after. Talk for hours, maybe a little hand graze here and there. Then he says, "I like you, but I'm not looking for anything serious."

We've all heard or used that statement before. But I feel that it's a huge, gigantic load of crap. It's not possible to control what's going to be "serious" or "not serious." That's to be decided by the experiences you have together in your relationship. There are way too many articles rolling around with rules about dating and how to find the right guy and who to date and who not to date.

If we all abided by the same rules and looked for the same thing, we'd all be trying to date the same person. And who wants to share her boyfriend?

No one (which is why the show *The Bachelor* is filled with drama).

So let's take a deep breath and light a match to all the rules about dating.

If you break up with your boyfriend and then meet a guy you really like only a week later, are you supposed to just let him pass you by? Or tell him that you "don't want anything serious" right now? You could do that, but you would be limiting yourself and potentially missing out on a great relationship.

I feel like people say they don't want anything serious if they meet someone post-breakup because that's what you're *supposed* to do. But we said no rules, remember? Saying you don't want anything serious is just a sissy way of protecting yourself. You're saying the pool is too cold when you haven't even felt the water yet.

Some guys have this way of thinking sometimes that all women want to rush things into a relationship where you're together all the time, have matching Halloween outfits, and flood each others profiles with cuddling pictures.

I'm in a relationship right now that you could say is pretty "serious." Last Halloween, we were Ron Burgundy and Veronica Corningstone from *Anchorman*. I flew to Wisconsin to meet his family for Christmas (negative 10 degrees outside). And we enjoy spending time together a lot.

However, it didn't just get this way in one week. It grew into a serious relationship over a year and a half. He enjoys it. I enjoy it. It *works*.

You can't force serious. On our first date, we didn't talk about what we were going to be for Halloween that year. It just happens over time. And I didn't have to read any dating rulebooks to get there. Someone who deems a relationship "unserious" from the start isn't worth your time. He or she is just afraid of the possibility that it could become serious down the road. People see friends all of the sudden flake out on plans and stop showing up because he or she is in a new relationship.

But people don't have to disappear from past lives when a boyfriend or girlfriend comes along, just learn to balance. And that's why it's so important for your friends to like your significant other so you can all hang out together and you don't have to choose between the two. But yes, if your friend is in a new relationship your friendship will probably change. However, if you're a good friend and you know that your friend is doing her best to balance, just be happy for her instead of focusing on the small changes in your friendship.

One thing you do have to realize, though, about college dating is that it moves a lot faster than high school dating.

With high school dating, maybe you see your boyfriend in between classes and then you meet at your locker at the end of the day. You hang out with him on the weekends, but there's usually some kind of supervision and usually no sleepovers.

In college, you're responsible for setting your own dating rules because there is little to no supervision to govern your decisions. Weekends aren't the only time to hang out anymore. Sometimes you'll be done with classes early or maybe you have a day where you don't have any classes scheduled. So, if you're in a relationship, you might be seeing a lot more of each other rather than waiting for the weekend.

This can escalate a relationship quickly. You have to remember to set your own terms and not get caught up in the "he's so dreamy" phase. Trust me, I've been there. Before you start labeling yourself as "taken" and clearing your schedule for him, ask yourself these questions …

1) How do I feel after I'm with him?
I know this sounds silly, but your feelings "post hangout" are really important. Do you feel good about yourself? Does he make you feel like you're the best thing in this world? He should. If you find yourself feeling down or insecure after you see him, that's red flag *numero uno*.

2) Do I like his friends?
Who he hangs out with is a big reflection of his values and his lifestyle. If all of his friends are smoking weed and skipping class, those aren't the kind of people you want to be around and that's definitely not the kind of influence you want on your significant other.

3) What do we do together?
The number one thing you don't want is a purely physical relationship. If he

knows the color of your underwear and not your goals and aspirations, drop him. Or, if you guys just don't have *fun* together. Do you just sit around and watch movies? Or do you go to sporting events and out with friends? Make sure that your time together doesn't just get "comfortable" where you feel like just each other is enough entertainment. It's not.

4) Does he believe in me?

After you hang out with him, do you want to run that 5K you were telling him about? He should make you feel like you can do anything in the world you want. If he told you you're not ready for a 5K, tell him he's ready for the highway. The person you're with should encourage you to be the best person you can be and never set limits on your goals.

5) Is he on your problem list?

If you spend more time worrying about him than you do enjoying him, it's time to move on. When you're with your friends, are you talking to them about how you're upset that he didn't call you last night? Or how you're worried about that girl he's always texting? One of the best pieces of relationship advice I ever got was this: A relationship should be an outlet to your problems, not one of your problems. Sure, every relationship has speed bumps here and there, but if it's becoming more of a worry and less of an enjoyment, what's the point? You don't have time for that.

Important note: My relationship advice applies to all people of every sexual orientation.

My Dream Internship

Katelynn Lee, James Madison University, Class of 2014

When I applied for my internship at TOMS, I checked over my application several times, crossed my fingers and gently pressed the 'send' button. I had wanted to intern and work for TOMS from the moment I heard about the mission of the company: to provide shoes for children in need. I remember I was teaching English in Peru and checking my e-mail after class when I was notified about the next steps for the interviewing process; I was ecstatic. After a few more interviews, I was on the next flight out to intern for TOMS.

When you work for something you believe in, work doesn't feel like work. When looking for jobs and future careers, it's easy to get distracted by numbers, benefits and paychecks. However, when you look at your life and how much of it you'll be working, don't you want to spend that time working for something you believe in?

Giving Back (Redefining Philanthropy)

College will get hectic. There will be times when you feel like you have so many tests and papers you can't breathe, or there will be a time when you feel like you're in too deep. This is also going to happen in life. You'll feel like your suffocating because your problems are so important and everyone should feel bad for you.

My solution to this is quite simple: philanthropy.

When you give back to others, you often feel like your problems aren't even problems at all.

However, when we hear the term "philanthropy," oftentimes we associate it with a requirement or something to cross off your list. Maybe you have service hours you have to complete for a club or maybe you're in a sorority and you have to raise X amount of dollars for an organization in order to get the points you need.

This isn't true philanthropy. When you're *required* to complete service hours, it takes away the best part.

It's great that schools want their students to give back, however with requirements we're sometimes programmed to think of the terms philanthropy and service as something on a checklist. We're so worried about crossing it off our list we forget the purpose behind it. We forget to feel that passion. I challenge all of you to redefine philanthropy from a requirement to a lifestyle. When you give back, you change your whole perspective on life. It makes you feel like you have no problems, and that's a great way to live.

As I have previously written, the company I started in college, Headbands of Hope, gives headbands to girls with cancer with every purchase. One day I was really mad at a tag company that messed up my order; I needed them for a show the following day. As I was pacing around my apartment yelling at them on the phone, an email popped up on my computer. A 15-year-old girl I had visited in the hospital the week before had just passed away. Her mom emailed me saying I had made such an impact on Taylor that she didn't take her headband off the whole week. Her mom wanted to get headbands for all the females in her family for her service that weekend because Taylor loved her headband so much.

At that moment, I didn't care about the tags. I didn't care about all the errands and meetings I had that day.

Everything in my mind had just been shuffled around and put in place, because I suddenly had a different perspective. This mother had just lost her daughter, and she thought to email me for headbands?

I didn't have a complaint in the world and I still don't (even though I need to remind myself sometimes).

If we can expose ourselves to areas of need and see how fortunate we are, what you think are problems usually aren't problems at all.

Think about your next service project. Maybe you have a dance marathon at your school. Instead of attending in order to get points for service hours or to hang out with your friends, get to know a family or a child you're benefitting beforehand. So, when you're dancing those long hours, you have a tangible connection to WHY you're dancing.

It's more than the points and the social aspect; you're changing a life.

Find a direct way to make a difference in a manner you can see right in front of you.

Don't do it to post on Facebook. Do it to make a difference.

Ways to Take Action	Causes You Care About		
	Cause 1	Cause 2	Cause 3
Action 1:			
Action 2:			
Action 3:			

Notes:

_____

_____

_____

_____

_____

_____

_____

PART 3: CAREER

Internships

It's never too early to start planning for your career. Sometimes we forget the purpose of college is to prepare us for post-graduation. Let's first start with internships …

The question isn't *if* you should do an internship, it's *when*. I can't even begin to express how internships shaped my career. If I didn't do the internships I did in college, I wouldn't be writing this book today. And therefore you would not be having a totally awesome Wednesday evening reading this book, right?

It all started my freshman year. I wish I could say I had been smart enough to start looking for internships my freshman year, but I kind of just fell into one.

Okay, I lied. I ran face-first into an internship to escape from campus.

It all started with a boy (most stories do, right?). We dated throughout high school and ended up going to the same college (not on purpose). We broke up in the middle of our first semester freshman year, but I kept seeing him everywhere because we had designed our schedules so we'd have some of the same classes (stupid decision on my part).

I was in mid-crisis when I saw a flyer for a semester internship at Disney World. At that point, the "happiest place on earth" sounded quite appealing. But what sounded more appealing was not seeing my ex for six months so I could move on.

I went to a Disney info session that night. I didn't really pay attention because I was busy picturing myself riding Space Mountain and eating ice cream in front of the Magic Kingdom.

The first part of the application was an online Q&A. Then, if you made it past that part, you had a phone interview (phone interview tips to come in the next chapter). A week after my phone interview, I was accepted to the program and packing my bags for Florida for six months. During my internship, I discovered the Make-A-Wish Foundation, which grants wishes to kids with life-threatening illnesses. I fell in love with the organization. Therefore, my sophomore year I interned at the Make-A-Wish Foundation of North Carolina. It was during my internship at Make-A-Wish that I became inspired to start my business, Headbands of Hope. Starting Headbands of Hope got the attention of the *TODAY Show* on NBC, and they offered me an internship for my junior year.

In my senior year, my business was booming so my department head granted me approval to "intern" for myself in order to fulfill my senior year internship requirement.

See what happened here? Every internship experience led into the next one. That's why it's important to start interning early in your college career. You learn firsthand about the field and/or the career you want to work in. You might find something you love, or you'll find something that leads you to something else.

You also get your feet wet and see if this career is even something you want to pursue. My career path totally changed based on my internship work. I originally thought I wanted to be a journalist, but I learned after interning at Make-A-Wish that I wanted to do something philanthropic as opposed to journalism.

Internships are becoming the new job market requirement. When you graduate, employers are looking for the types of hands-on experiences you had in college. I would argue that your GPA isn't as important as the work-related experiences you had.

You'll hear people tell you that your junior and senior years are for internships because you're more "knowledgeable" about your field. However, I say that couldn't be more wrong.

Start early. Your experiences early in college will open more doors for you towards the end of your college career. I may have not gotten my internship at Make-A-Wish if I didn't have my internship in Disney World before. And more importantly, I wouldn't have known that I even wanted to intern with Make-A-Wish if I didn't intern at Disney.

Internships are kind of like dating. Relationships show you what you like and what you don't like in a significant other. Maybe you're always going after the same type of guy: the "bad boy." You date the guy that texts but *never* calls. Or the one that honks when he's in your driveway. But then one day, you go on a date with a different guy that comes to your door and brings you flowers and calls to tell you goodnight. Now, you learn that maybe you don't want the "bad boy" after all because you saw what else is out there.

Believe it or not, this scenario can also be applied to your career.

The more opportunities you have to involve yourself in hands-on work experience, the more you'll know about what you like and what you don't like in a job. You may think you have the perfect plan for your career and know what you want to do, but you don't really know until you give it a shot. Internships are the perfect opportunity to test out the work you may or may not want to do.

When it's time to apply for a full-time job after college, you'll feel more confident about your career choice because you've already gotten your feet wet. Additionally, the professional experience you've had with internships will always help landing a job.

Although it helps if you have had an internship in the same kind of business or career you're applying for, it isn't completely necessary. For example, let's look at my past internship. After working at Disney World, I knew I didn't want to work there full time or even do anything related to parks and recreation or tourism. However, I had learned from the best customer service provider in the world (in my opinion). I learned how to shake hands, how to welcome customers, how to make people feel appreciated, how to deal with customer issues and I even learned how to point (point with two fingers or a full hand, pointing with one finger can be too "harsh").

I applied everything I learned about customer service at Disney World into subsequent internships. I especially applied all that I had learned into my company, which has become my full-time job. Even if you intern at an event planning company and you realize you actually want to work in politics, you still can use the organizing and delegating skills you learned in event planning and channel them into politics. No internship or experience is a waste. If you learned from it, it's a success.

Picking an Internship

Local businesses relevant to your career:

1.

2.

3.

Companies you admire (do not have to be local or relevant to your major):

1.

2.

3.

Finding An Internship:

Now that I've officially ingrained in your brain to do internships (hence the plural), let's talk about where to look and how to get them.

Here are 3 ways to find an internship ...

1) Meet with your advisor.
Request a meeting with your academic advisor to discuss internships. The reason why you should start with your advisor is because he or she is specific to your major and has experience with past students who have completed internships.

A lot of companies like hiring from the same school every time, especially if they're local. Therefore, your advisor can help connect you with internship oppurtunities where previous students in your major have completed.

2) Go to your career center.
This is what these centers are made for. Take advantage of them. Career centers provide resources and assistance, which would normally cost a chunk of cash to get outside of college.

Sometimes it can be hard to get an appointment because seniors who are panicking near graduation line up at the door at the career center. So be sure to schedule an appointment early in the semester to avoid graduation rush.

Another reason to go to the career center early (as a freshman) is because they get to know you and remember you. Keep in mind: the people that work in the career center are the ones with the job connections. If you make an appearance your freshman year and form an ongoing relationship with the counselors for all four years they're more likely to help you get a job your senior year.

Even if you haven't declared a major yet and you have no earthly clue what you want to do, go to the career center. Request assistance with finding an internship, which could, in the future, be applied to different career paths. For example, interning at a non-profit or interning in a customer service position at a company can be applied to different careers like sales, management, or finance. Just because you don't know what you want to do doesn't mean you should wait for a light bulb to pop into your head. The easiest way to find your path is to just start walking.

3) Be bold.
If you've met with your advisor and career center and nothing pops, then it's time for my favorite plan. Take on the task yourself.

Find businesses you admire or a cause you care about. Find a phone number or go directly to their office. Even if they don't have any internship listings on their websites, it doesn't mean one can't be created for you.

If you go the phone route, this is what you should do …

Go to the directory on a company's website and find a person's name in the position that interests you. For example, if you're calling a non-profit and you're interested in the fundraising side, call the fundraising director.

Here's an example of how the conversation should go …

Company: Hello, this is <u>name</u>. How can I help you?

You: Hi, <u>name</u>. My name is <u>your name</u> and I'm a student at <u>university name here</u>. I'm very interested in helping with the mission of <u>company name here.</u> Is now a good time for you to talk?

(Always ask if now is a good time to talk, whoever you call)

Company: Oh, sure. I have a few minutes.

You: Thanks so much. I've developed an interest in the fundraising side of non-profits. I see you have your annual fundraiser coming up in a few months. I'd love to assist you and take some tasks off your plate. Would you like to meet for coffee and discuss this possibility?

Hence, you're not asking the fundraising director to teach you anything, because that would mean taking time away from his or her job. You're goal is to make this person feel that you're going to make his or her job easier, without any handholding.

When you land an in-person meeting with this person, bring a résumé and any examples of past work you've done. *Always* thank him or her at the beginning for meeting with you. Do your research on the company. For example, in this scenario, come with specifics about the fundraiser and how you can help.

You: I see you had local businesses come out last year to sponsor. I'd be happy to approach more businesses to come on board for the fundraiser this year.

What you don't want to do is say, "I want to help" and not back it up with any ideas.

One of my pet peeves with my company is when people take my time to talk to me about helping or interning, and they bring nothing to the table for me to consider.

What differentiates being an intern and being an amazing intern is not waiting for tasks to be assigned to you, it's creating tasks without help, getting approval, and executing them.

It becomes a task itself to come up with tasks for an intern to do. Therefore, busy work is often correlated with internships.

Bottom line: When asking for an internship, make your argument by speaking about how *you* can benefit the company, not how they can benefit you.

That brings me to my next point … interviewing.

Notes:

_____

_____

_____

_____

_____

_____

_____

_____

_____

_____

Interviewing

Just the word "interview" gives people the jitters. Sure, there's a lot riding on one short conversation, but that doesn't mean you shouldn't walk in there with the upmost confidence.

However, a lot of companies opt for the phone interview first. This is a way of weeding out in-person interviews. It's important to nail it so you can move forward to an office interview.

Here are some tips for phone interviews:

- Make sure you know who's calling whom. Are you supposed to call the interviewer at the specified time, or is he or she supposed to call you?

- Double-check the time zone for the call. I've missed phone meetings because I forgot to convert the time zone. Don't make the same mistake I did!

- Go to a quiet spot with good reception! One way to fail an interview is if the interviewer can't hear you. It shows you're not prepared when there's background noise or bad reception. Use a landline when you can. Put a note on your door so your roommates don't try to come in. I have a headset I use for Skype calls or interviews so I know I sound crisp and clear.

- Have your computer in front of you with Google pulled up. It's always good to have web access prepared for a phone interview in case you need to quickly look something up. Have the company's website pulled up in your browser to have facts in front of you. However, don't become distracted by your computer or look up every question, just use it for emergency purposes. Take advantage of the fact that the interviewer can't see you.

- Turn off phone features. With smart phones today, you can do anything. Customize your phone so you can't hear call waiting or texts coming in. They'll distract you.

- Have a physical copy of your résumé and the job description in front of you. Therefore, if nerves strike and you forget some of your qualifications or specifics of the job, both will be right in front of you.

- Answer the phone by saying your name, "Hello, this is (your name here)." Saying your name when you answer shows you're professional and also confirms to the interviewer that he or she has the right person.

- Smile when you talk. Even though the interviewer can't see you, your tone sounds more positive when you smile.

- Don't ramble. Sometimes in phone interviews it's hard to know when to start talking and when to stop talking because you can't body language. Therefore, it's easy to ramble and get off topic. Sometimes, an interviewer will be writing down your answers so there might be a pause after you've finished talking. Don't try to fill that pause, let them write. Answer the question clearly and concisely, and try to add a closing sentence so the interviewer knows it's the end of your answer.

- Try to get an in-person meeting, whether it's an office meeting or a cup of coffee. Meeting with someone face-to-face shows your interest in the position and gives him or her a better sense of your qualities as a person.

- Follow up immediately with an email, then a few days later with a hand-written note. Always follow up an interview with a nice note thanking them for their time and leaving your door open for further conversation. If you were asked about something in the interview, like writing samples, send those along with your follow up. Always send another follow up with a *hand-written* letter. It shows your desire for the position because you took the time to personalize and mail a letter.

Now that we've discussed phone interview tips, let's assume you moved forward to an in-person interview (which obviously you will).

A few of the above points will carry over into an in-person interview, but there's more that goes into it than that.

First step: appearance.

I know the saying: "It's not about what's on the outside. It's what's on the inside that really counts."

I respectfully disagree. How you present yourself is a form of respect. Of course, it's important to have the heart and passion for what you do. However, what you choose to wear says a lot about you, which is why it's important, especially for an interview.

Don't wear your brightest colors. For an interview, you want to be neutral and professional. Leave the hot pink and yellow for a night out with your friends.

Do stick with the blacks, greys, whites, creams and navy blues. Like I said, keep it neutral and professional. You don't want to be "that girl" walking into the office with a hot pink dress and heels. However (allow me to be gross for a second), think ahead of how your outfit will handle sweat. I know that I sweat under my arms when I'm nervous. Therefore, I don't wear grey tops because sweat shows on them. Just a tip of advice you most likely won't get from *Vogue*.

Don't show cleavage or much skin. Make sure your top is high enough so there is zero opportunity for cleavage distraction. And make sure your skirt is long enough—to at least the knee. If you wear a skirt, wear tights under it, even if they're nude stockings. Bare legs can be unprofessional. If you're going to wear pants, make sure they're actually pants and not capris. Capris, even if they're khaki or nice material, aren't professional.

Do iron your clothes beforehand. The quickest way to create a bad first-impression is by coming in with a wrinkly shirt or trousers. It shows you're unprepared and were probably rushed in the morning or didn't look in the mirror. Always leave time to iron your clothes. Even better, iron or steam them the night before.

Don't do the messy bun. It might be cute for lunch with friends or at the gym, but don't do it for an interview. Again, it looks like you rushed and didn't leave time for your hair.

Do keep your hair out of your face. Whether it's pinned back in a sleek ponytail or sprayed out of the way, make sure it's not covering your face, especially your eyes. The most annoying thing occurs when I'm talking to a person and I want to tuck his or her hair behind an ear. Major distraction.

Don't wear overly-large or showy jewelry. No dangly earrings or super chunky necklaces. Earring studs and/or a simple necklace is enough. If you like to wear multiple rings or stack bangles, leave those at home. Too much jewelry can be distracting. Leave it to one or two simple pieces.

Do be comfortable. The last thing you want to be doing is tugging at your shirt or stopping circulation when you sit down in your pencil skirt. The more comfortable you are the more relaxed you'll be and the better you'll perform.

Do invest in a sleek purse/briefcase. Don't bring your oversized flower bag. Find something simple that can carry a laptop and a notepad.

I know this seems like a lot of rules, and you're not "expressing" yourself with these strict guidelines. But your goal with an outfit for an interview is to have it be the least distracting as possible. You want the interviewer to concentrate on you and your words, not your outfit.

Leave the "expressing yourself" to the interview conversation.

Now that we have the outfit figured out, let's move onto preparation.

Here are some tips to prepare for the interview (phone or in-person) ...

1) Know everything you can about the company you're applying for.

These are questions you should be able to answer ...

- How did the company start? Founder? Year?
- What's the mission of the company?
- What events do they hold?
- Who are the big wigs? (Know the names of the CEOs, directors, etc.)
- What are the tasks/goals involved in your position?
- What are their markets? Biggest clients?

Obviously these questions vary based on the company or organization, but you get the picture. The reason why it's important to know all the details about the company is because you want to be able to drop these facts at various points during the interview to show you're prepared.

This is what differentiates an average interview from a great interview:

Average:

Interviewer: What is your biggest strength?
Interviewee: I'd say I'm really great at talking to people. I was president of my sorority and I used my people skills during rush and other events.

Great:

Interviewer: What is your biggest strength?
Interviewee: Although I don't like to brag, I've been told I'm great with people. As president of my sorority, I used my networking and communication skills to make us one of the most admirable chapters on campus. With your 20th Annual Gala coming up this March, I know I could use this strength to increase sponsorships and ticket sales. In addition, I'd be a wonderful door greeter for the night of the event.

See the difference here? Catering your answer to a specific company can change their opinion of you drastically (for the better, of course).

Anyone can answer what his or her biggest strength is, or anyone can answer what their past work experience is, but not just anyone can explain how their answers can help that company *specifically*. Not just any company, the specific company you're interviewing for. That's why it's important to know the company inside and out.

Also, they could definitely ask you questions about the company to test your knowledge. That's another reason to study their website like it's your final exam.

2) Another way to prepare is by studying your own résumé and recounting all of your experiences. Sometimes, when you're in the heat of an interview, you forget to mention that time you directed your school's community service day or your recent election as president of your club.

Don't just memorize your accomplishments. Think about how you can translate those accomplishments into career related work. If you won your school's creative writing contest, translate that into thinking outside the box and bringing your creative side to company projects.

3) Before you go into the office, write a hand-written note thanking the interviewer for his or her time and consideration. Seal it and drop it off at the receptionist after your interview, and ask him or her to kindly deliver it to your interviewer. This shows you're on top of your game. For an interviewer to receive a handwritten note the same day as the interview makes a huge statement.

4) Print out a hard copy of your résumé and any other materials you can give them: writing samples, graphic design work you've done, or any other work that can show your skill.

5) Practice a mock interview with your friends, family or career center. It might sound silly, but it helps to practice beforehand, especially if you're new to interviewing. Comb through your answers and practice answering absurd questions.

It's very common to be asked crazy questions in an interview. Your ability to answer them shows you can think on your feet.

Once I was asked, "If you could be any fruit, which fruit would you be?"

My answer: "I'd be a banana because the potassium prevents cramping and I like to prevent problems before they happen." Good, right?

I know a guy who always asks people he interviews how many Walmarts there are in the United States.

The position their interviewing for is marketing, so why do they care how many Walmarts there are in the country? Because it shows your ability to think logically and problem solve.

If your answer is 20, you probably didn't think about it clearly. But if you said, "let's assume there are 5 Walmarts per state, and there are 50 states, so 50 times 5 is 250. So I'm going to go with 250 Walmarts."

Whether or not that answer is accurate (it's actually 4,177) it doesn't matter. What matters is how the interviewee demonstrated his or her problem solving and the ability to think logically.

Accordingly, practice answering any kind of questions you can. The important part is to answer the question. Don't sit there like a deer in headlights.

6) Come up with questions to ask the interviewer.

99% of the time, the interviewer will close with: "Do you have any questions for me?"

This portion of the interview is equally as important as the answers you give to the questions they ask.

The questions you ask can show your desire for the job and how much you care about the position.

Here are examples of good questions to ask.

- "How would you describe the company's culture here?"
- "What would you say are the three most important skills needed for this position?"
- "What does success look like in this job?"
- "Is this a new position or did someone else hold it previously?"
- "What's the biggest problem facing this company, and will I be in a position to help?"
- "What are the next steps? When will you be making a decision?"

Don't ask:

- "What are my vacation days?"
- "Can I take personal phone calls during the day?"

- "Where will my office be and will there be a window?"
- "Do the staff lunches have vegetarian options?"
- "Do you do background checks? Drug testing?"
- "Do you monitor all emails?"

And never ask anything that's public knowledge about the company (AKA could be found on *Google)*.

Save all salary and benefits questions for after you're offered the job.

Don't be afraid to write them down on your notebook and refer to them when the time comes.

7) Invest in business cards. Never leave an interview without offering your card.

8) Bring a notepad. Take notes whenever you're given details or anything specific. Taking notes shows you're not taking this opportunity for granted and you're prepared.

9) Drive to the interview location the day before to ensure you can find the building and know the parking situation. The last thing you want is to get lost and be late. Make sure you know exactly where you're going.

Notes:

_____

_____

_____

_____

_____

_____

_____

_____

_____

_____

_____

_____

_____

_____

_____

_____

The Actual Interview

If you have a morning interview, get up at least two hours before so you can be fully awake. You do not want to look tired. Maybe go for a run and definitely eat a well-balanced breakfast.

Arrive at least 10-15 minutes early. It's better to be early than late. On time is considered late, trust me. Don't push it.

Turn *off* your cell phone. Not vibrate, off.

Don't freak out. Take deep breaths and remember why you're awesome and qualified for this job. Your preparation will ease the nerves.

When they call you in, smile and be excited.

Shake the interviewer's hand. One of my biggest pet peeves is a weak handshake. It's a huge turnoff to a lot of professionals. I'd rather you break my wrist than give me a sloppy fish handshake.

Look the interviewer in the eyes. Give him or her a firm, two-pump handshake, and say their name in your greeting. Start with using a prefix in front to show respect.

"Mr. Sullivan, thank you so much for meeting with me."

If they correct you and say, "Please, call me Dan." Then call him Dan.

*Make sure you research and see if the interviewer has a doctorate. Don't call Dan "Mr. Sullivan" if he's "Dr. Sullivan."

People like to hear their name. It's as simple as that. Use his or her name whenever possible.

Example:

Interviewer: What's your favorite thing about working in sales?
You: That's a great question, Dan. (then continue with your answer)

Saying a person's name makes the interview more personalized.

An important thing to remember is that interviewing can be uncomfortable and awkward on *both* ends. I've been on both sides as the interviewer and the interviewee. Do whatever you can to make the situation more comfortable.

Don't be afraid to start the interview with a personal conversation. If you see a picture of a dog on the desk and you're a dog-lover, ask what kind of dog he or she has. Making an interview into a conversation is more enjoyable on both ends. Therefore, when you leave, the interviewer will feel more positive about the interview if it was enjoyable.

And lets face it; almost everyone likes talking about him or herself. If you see a degree on the wall, ask the interviewer what it was like to go to school in Miami or Washington. They want to break the ice as much as you do.

Throughout the interview, maintain proper body language. Keep your legs crossed, sit up straight. Basically, everything your mom told you to do at dinner.

Try to steer away from nervous habits like tapping your foot or playing with your hair or giggling too much. Just be calm, cool and collected.

When it's coming to an end and it's time to ask your questions, refer to your notepad. It shows you really took the time to think about this position and the company.

Usually, he or she will give you some sort of timeline when they'll make their decision. If they don't, ask when you can expect to be notified about the job.

When leaving, stand up and shake the interviewer's hand. *Say his or her name* again.

"Thank you so much for the opportunity, Dan. I hope to hear from you soon and here's my card if you need anything else to help with your decision."

Never ask for someone's card. They'll give it to you if they want to keep in touch.

Drop your thank-you note off at the desk.

Take 24 hours to send a follow up email.

Example of a good follow up email …

Hi (name here),

I wanted thank you again for meeting with me yesterday. After meeting with you, I'm even more excited about the possibility of working for (insert company name).

I also wanted to attach a couple of the writing samples we talked about yesterday.

Thank you again for the consideration and please let me know if there's anything you need to help you in your decision.

(signature)

Notes:

_____

_____

_____

_____

_____

_____

_____

_____

_____

_____

_____

_____

_____

_____

_____

_____

Getting Rejected

It's going to happen. There will be times where you're rejected and maybe you didn't get the job you wanted or you didn't win the election for student council president. But one of the most important things to take away from this book is that *rejection is a good thing*. In fact, I'd argue if you're too comfortable and not getting rejected, you're not reaching high enough.

I get rejected everyday. In the beginning, it hurt. But now I've reached a point where rejection fuels me to go even further.

I owe my successes to the people who told me no. Because those no's mean that I'm trying. And the more you try, the more chances you have to get a yes.

Sure, I got a no from Lucy Hale to wear Headbands of Hope. But after I got that no, I got a yes from Lauren Conrad, Zooey Deschanel, Amy Poehler, Jessica Alba, PINK, and Katy Perry.

Once you get over the fear of getting rejected, your life becomes way better and more of an adventure. You'd be surprised how many times you think you'll get rejected and don't. One time I got to sit in first class on a flight because I just asked if there were any empty seats available. One time I got extra sprinkles on my frozen yogurt because I asked for them. See what being fearless can get you? First class and sprinkles.

What would happen if they said no? I'd be sitting in coach and only have one forth of the sprinkles I wanted. Life goes on.

If you get rejected from an internship, don't let it discourage you. Use it as fuel to move forward. However, if you get rejected from an internship you believe you really want, don't give up on it.

Follow up with them periodically throughout the semester. Keep tabs on the company and if anything happens, like they have an event or they hit a milestone, send them a congratulatory email. This shows you're still invested in the company and on top of your game. Politely request another shot at the internship for the following semester. You'd be surprised what a little relationship building can do over the course of a semester.

As a freshman, I interviewed for an internship with the V Foundation for Cancer Research. I was declined because they said they only allow juniors and seniors to intern. I periodically followed up throughout my freshman and sophomore years and sent them *handwritten* holiday cards.

In my junior year I already had another internship, but the V Foundation called me asking if I was still interested in the position. They offered me an internship after two years of not seeing me because I didn't let them forget me.

Just because you get a no from someone doesn't mean you can't turn it into a yes eventually. Never give up on something you truly want.

Rejection is just a sign that you're on the right track because you're challenging yourself. No matter how many times you're told "no," you're still a mile ahead of everyone sitting on the couch.

Notes:

When You Get a Bite

The more you put yourself out there, the better chance you have of landing an internship. Don't put all of your eggs in one basket and hope that you get the only one you applied for. Put your résumé in a lot of different hands so you have options.

But when you do nail an internship, get ready to work. Request a meeting with your supervisor on the first day (if he or she hasn't already done so), and go over what's expected of you short-term and long-term. Just like you did in the interview phase, come prepared with questions the first day.

When we think of internships, it's often connected to tiny tasks like getting coffee or licking envelopes. But an important thing to realize is that you'll only be filling coffee if you haven't proved yourself otherwise.

Allow me to give you an example …

One summer I was interning at the *TODAY Show*. The executive director came in every morning and picked an intern to get his breakfast sandwich from across the street. "Wheat bread, turkey bacon, egg whites and hot sauce. Don't forget the hot sauce," he'd say.

One day, he chose my friend Hannah to get the sandwich. As she was leaving the sandwich place she turned around to the cashier and said, "Just to double-check, there's hot sauce on this?"

"Actually I totally forgot. Here, let me add some."

Hannah turned around and slammed the sandwich on the counter. She looked him in the eyes and said, "My *life* depends on whether or not there is hot sauce on this sandwich. FIX IT." Scenarios like this are the reason why we think of filling coffee cups, adding one-and-a-half Splenda packets, and organic creamer when we hear the word "intern."

However, your internship doesn't have to be licking envelopes and doing coffee runs. If that's your only worth to them, then you're probably not doing a very good job as an intern. This goes back to what I said before about waiting for tasks to come to you. If you wait for tasks to be handed to you, you're going to get the crappy, unimportant, mindless tasks.

Prove to your supervisor that you can handle the professional tasks. Actually, prove to him or her that you cannot only *handle* the professional tasks, but you're good at them. Offer to draft a press release for the upcoming event. Create a list of social media campaign ideas that could be used. Speak up with ideas in the next staff meeting. You might draft ten press releases before your boss actually uses one; but it shows that you're dedicated and hardworking.

I used to pitch ideas all the time at the *TODAY Show*. Ninety-nine percent of the time they'd get shut down. Until one day I was in a staff meeting and the executive director concluded with "any other ideas?"

I raised my hand and said I heard of a robot that always wins in the game rock, paper, and scissors because it can anticipate what move you're about throw.

The next day, that robot was on the *TODAY Show*.

That was the only pitch they took of mine all summer, but I was the only intern to get an idea televised because I was the only one that really tried.

This brings me to …

How To Turn An Internship Into a Job

This is my favorite challenge.

Let's face it, what's the point of doing internships anyway? Yes, to get hands-on experience. But in the end, we're looking for that job offer. Internships are not only beneficial for you to test-drive a career; they're beneficial for your employer to see what your skills really are on a more in-depth level than just an interview and resume. He or she gets to see you in action. So what's the trick to getting that offer at the end of your internship?

One word: irreplaceable.

Make yourself worth something to the company. Add value to the position you're in, and you'll be irreplaceable. If you're just stuck doing busy work, they can find someone else to fill your shoes in two seconds. But, if you're bringing new ideas to the company or increasing their following on social media, you're adding value as an employee. You know you have value when you leave your internship to go back to school and the company feels that it's missing "something."

What they're missing is *you*.

I've had quite a few interns with Headbands of Hope. Most of them were replaceable ... except for one.

My first ever hire with my company was an intern that blew my socks off. She started as a campus representative at her school. Fast forward a couple months down the road, she was head of all the campus reps in the nation.

Eventually I stopped giving her tasks because she was so good at creating her own tasks that I didn't want to waste her efforts on things I could have my assistant do.

As an intern, she was my go-to person for events or any networking opportunities I couldn't make. She gained my trust; I encouraged her to be the face of the company when I couldn't.

Needless to say, she was hired immediately following her graduation. When an employer finds someone who's irreplaceable, the company has a very hard time letting the intern float away, whether there's a position available or not. Even if the company isn't hiring at the time, they'll make room for someone who proves his or her value.

Here are some steps to get hired during an internship:

- **Arrive early:** I know this seems simple, but being there before your boss walks in everyday says a lot about your work ethic. Notice how I didn't say, "Leave late." I don't think leaving late says as much as coming in early. I appreciate employees who find efficient and effective ways to do their work and don't need to work into the night. Arrive early and work efficiently.

- **Don't wait for tasks:** If you wait for tasks to come to you, you'll most likely get the stereotypical "intern" ones: filling coffee, licking envelopes, or making cold calls. But, if you take initiative and create your own tasks, you prove yourself as a "real" employee and your supervisors can see your value. If you take the initiative and put some great ideas together for their annual fundraiser, your next task will probably not include filling coffee … unless it's coffee for you because of all the professional tasks that were just handed to you.

- **Make your work measureable:** It's one thing to come into an interview and say you're 'good at social media' or you 'work really hard.' It's a whole other ballgame when you come into an interview with numerical evidence of growth on a social media account or an exact number of revenue growth you brought during an internship. Opinions about you can't always be trusted. Numbers don't lie.

- **Make it known:** Lastly, make it known that you want the job. You won't be considered for the job if you don't seem like you want to work there. Request a meeting with your boss in the middle of your internship. Explain how much you believe in the company and what they do. Then, have measurable evidence of the work you've done, and express your interest in a position at the company post-graduation. If they say they're not hiring or "We'll see," ask what steps you can take now to prepare yourself to come on full-time.

Social Media and Your Career

The fact that you're reading this book means you care about your future and your career. Therefore, I'm going to assume you're smart enough to know the *obvious* things *not* to put on your social media that could jeopardize your career.

Obviously don't do this:

- A picture of you doing a keg stand (or any crazy partying)
- A picture of you holding a solo cup or any underage drinking
- A tweet about how hung-over you are
- Bashing your boss (or a coworker)
- Bashing the company you work for

Now that we have the obvious out of the way, there are still some things to be careful with on your social media. Sure, it's an avenue to express who you are, but what you say and what you post could put your career at risk and you may not even know it.

Maybe not so obvious:

- Posting strong political or religious statements: You're free to have your own political and religious opinions and beliefs. Everyone is. But social media can be a very dangerous way to express these. Remember that everyone has the freedom to believe what he or she wants, and it's not your place to try to sway him or her otherwise. And it's *definitely* not going to work to change someone's mind by posting an angry Facebook post about how stupid our government is or reasons why Christianity is wrong. These are definite red zones on social media and should be confined to your own head and/or discussed only with close family/friends.

- Talking about skipping class or not studying for a test: Do you think someone would want to hire you if they saw you weren't prepared for a test? And not just that you weren't prepared, but that you *gave* out that information freely through your social media. Meaning, that you wanted to show the world your apathy towards school. It might not seem detrimental, but it's certainly not going to help you.

How social media can help you in your career:

- Posting pictures of you doing super cool or charitable things. Did you hike one of the highest peaks in America? Post it. Did you dance your heart out at your dance marathon? Post it. Did you spend your weekend at a leadership retreat? Post it. When employers check your profile (which they will, even after you got the job) you want to show them what an awesome person you are outside of the workplace, as well.
- Social media makes it super easy to stay connected with people (AKA network). The more you can communicate and keep up with friends and family, the more opportunities you can become aware of. If a company is looking for a new sales rep, the person doing the hiring will most likely post it to Facebook.
- If your posts are getting a lot of likes or you have a lot of Twitter followers, it shows that people are interested in you and what you say. That's an attractive quality to an employer because they can see that you have a strong network and work well with people.

LinkedIn

If you don't have a LinkedIn, get one. Even if you don't really use it, it's good to see that you show up when someone searches your name. Copy and paste your résumé and find a good headshot and you're good to go.

Once you start job searching, try to make connections on LinkedIn with people you know so you can start seeing what's out there, and start conversations with potential employers.

Twitter and Instagram

What's your username? If it's xohotbunnyxo, it might be time to change that. Make sure you choose something professional.

Tip: Always assume that your boss is reading your social media accounts. Just because he or she isn't active on social media, doesn't mean they're not monitoring your accounts.

Starting a Business In College

When we're approaching graduation, it feels like we only have two options: get a job or grad school. But the third option of entrepreneurship should be more visible.

I started my company, Headbands of Hope, when I was a junior in college at the age of nineteen. One of the biggest mistakes I made in the beginning was that I hid the fact that I was in college. I thought that having conference calls in between Spanish class and PE101 would make me seem less credible.

However, I was so wrong. I learned that college was actually a brilliant time to start something you believe in, whether it's a business, a non-profit or a club on campus. Here are some reasons why ...

1) Crush "20 something" stereotypes ...

Let's face it, we all know the stereotypes of the millennial generation: lazy, facebooking, twerking 20-somethings who don't know hard work. A lot of society loves to believe that stereotype. Therefore, when a millennial does something awesome, it's a big deal. So much of the press and attention I got when I founded my company was because I was so young. Sometimes, it's the whole angle of the story, "young people doing big things." Use your young age to your advantage. Be proud to be a millennial.

2) Professors = Mentors …

When I got the idea for Headbands of Hope, I didn't have a business degree or know anything about manufacturing a product. All I had was the inspiration and a few seconds of courage to decide to go for it. And then I came to a wonderful realization: I'm surrounded by experts. When you're on a college campus, professors, filled with knowledge and experience, can help you. Most professors want to see you succeed in and out of the classroom. I met with business professors that I never had as teachers. I was just a student at the university and they wanted to help me succeed by answering my questions. All of the logistics of starting a business and everything else I was afraid of were answered because I was a student.

3) Numbers …

When you're a college student, you don't just have the support of professors, you have the support of students. If you've ever been to a university football game or any kind of large school event, you'll witness a sea of students uniting behind one thing, which is pretty cool. It doesn't matter if you know each other or not, students want people at his or her university to succeed and do great things. My first big market was students at NCSU. And then those students told their friends and family, and then my mission started having a ripple effect across the country (and even internationally now). The point is a college campus is filled with support. When starting a business or starting any project, you need strong support to get the wheels turning. Take advantage of being on a college campus to get your idea rolling.

4) Less responsibility …

In college, you have responsibility, however probably not as much as you will when you graduate and you're in the "real world." Most likely, you don't have kids, you don't have a mortgage or anyone else to support. It's just you and your life. You have the ability to choose yourself and be selfish. Invest heart, soul and bank account into something that you believe in. When there's less responsibility for you to worry about, it's easier to take these kinds of risks.

5) It's okay to fail ...

We've already talked about taking failures as opportunities. Even if you start a business and it fails, you learn a lot.

If you mess up at something while you're in college, there's still so much room to bounce back. The last thought you want after college is the regret from not going after a dream.

I've found when things don't go as planned (which is very frequent) it's called an experience. Experiences are carried with you the rest of your life, giving you more insight to the world around you.

My point isn't about starting a company in college that will turn into your full-time job or make you super rich or famous. My point is about using the resources available to you in that 4 years (or 5 ... or 6) and creating experiences.

If You Don't Want To Start a Business

That's totally cool, too. There are still other ways to gain experience and earn money while you're a student. Sure, waitressing might help you pay the bills, but it's not exactly making your résumé jump. Instead, try to get a job that you can channel into the professional world.

Here are some of my suggestions:

Visitor's Center:
Working at the university's visitor's center is a great way to gain professional social skills. During the busy season, you could be greeting hundreds of people per day and answering questions about the university. You might even do some public speaking to groups, which is always great to put on your résumé.

Customer Service:
I did customer service for a few semesters at our school gym. I was at the front desk greeting people and answering questions or problems. I could have easily translated my desk job at the gym to working in customer service for another company.

Journalist:
Writing for your school paper is a no-brainer if you're going into a career that involves writing or researching. Not only will you get paid per article, you're building an awesome portfolio to present to a future employer.

Student Activities Board:

Sometimes this is a club and sometimes these are paid positions, so you'll just have to figure out which one it is on your campus. Either way, working on the activities board helps you gain professional experience in event planning. Whether you want to go into event planning or not, having examples of projects and events that you built and spearheaded from the ground up is a great demonstration of your work ethic.

Tutor:

A lot of campuses have tutoring services where they employ students who excel at certain subjects. I was never exceptionally good at any particular subject, or else I totally would have done this. You can get paid (pretty good money sometimes) to help students with their homework and/or projects. Having this on a résumé not only shows you excelled academically, it shows your ability to explain concepts clearly, which is always a good skill to have.

Notes:

_____

_____

_____

_____

_____

_____

_____

PART 4: DO IT FOR YOU

Find Your Own Success

In the end, college is about you. It's about using your resources to grow into the person you want to be. It's not about what your parents want you to do; it's not what a BuzzFeed quiz said you should be. It's about you.

This means you have to dig deep and really think about what *you* want and what's important to you. I know it sounds simple, but eliminating third party influences can be challenging. It's not easy to ignore people telling you you're a great writer so you *have* to be a journalist.

But do you want to be a journalist? Just because you're good at something, doesn't mean you have to make a career out of it.

We often hear people say, "do what you love," which is true to a certain extent. But I love hiking and I also love cookies. Realistically, I don't think those are great options for a career. What we love can simply just be enjoyments in our lives and we don't have to force those enjoyments into a career. Instead of focusing on finding something you love, find your definition of success.

What will success feel like to you?

I guarantee right now, success won't come from a paycheck, a job title, or any tangible achievement. Those are all great milestones in your life, but they won't fill your heart with success (as much as you think that next promotion will do the trick).

That's the never-ending trap we find ourselves in. We're always reaching for the next thing in hopes that it's the final puzzle piece to our happiness. I can be guilty of this, as well. I'll tell myself, "As soon as Headbands of Hope is on the *TODAY Show*, then I'll be content." But then Headbands of Hope was on the *TODAY Show* and it was a great moment in my life, but that's all it was: a moment. Then it was over.

When I go to the hospital and I give a headband to a girl who just lost her hair to chemotherapy and I see her smile after she looks in the mirror, that's more than a moment. That's a time in my life that isn't ever over; it's infused in everything I do.

From that moment on, everything I do is reaching towards recreating that moment for all girls with cancer because I know what success feels like to me. If you're not sure what success is to you, remember one thing: success is not an award, it's a feeling.

Imagine yourself waking up everyday. What will get you out of bed in the morning? Coffee can only do so much. You have to have an element of excitement in your work and that comes from finding purpose in it. That sounds weird, so let me elaborate.

Remember those crazy math classes where we had to learn and memorize lots of crazy equations? When you were studying, you'd get frustrated because you'd be like, "When am I *ever* going to use this?"

That's exactly what you don't want to happen at your job. You need to know why you're doing what you're doing, and you need to feel it's important. If you're working for a company and you feel your role serves no purpose, then you feel no purpose.

But here's the thing, this doesn't mean that you can only be satisfied with a "powerful" title, like director of a department or CEO of a company. When I interned at Make-A-Wish, I wasn't calling Taylor Swift or throwing huge magical parties. Usually, I was calling doctors offices and getting medical forms and making sure the wish child and his or her family were cleared to go on their wish. Even though it may not have been glamorous and exciting,

I knew *why* I was doing what I was doing and I knew it was important. Therefore, I loved my job.

The career you choose doesn't have to be directly cause-related (like working for a non-profit) in order to be a fulfilling career. Your fulfillment comes from finding your purpose in a job and feeling it's important. For example, if you decide to go into construction, don't do it to just build homes; create safe environments for future families. Or if you decide to go into engineering, don't do it to just create technology, challenge the status quo and revolutionize the future. If you want to go into advertising, create campaigns for brands you believe in.

See what I'm getting at?

Look past the job title until you can see the meaning of your role and what your life will look like in it. Instead of looking for a job in order to find success, find your definition of success and then find a job that will help you get there.

Establish Personal Goals

Feeling inspired? Feeling super excited about college and the rest of your life? Good, I've done my job. Now, before you do *anything* else, write it down. Don't save this for later. Don't go grab a Diet Coke before you start. Write. It. Down.

Inspiration can fade, written goals can't. When you write something down, it also makes it more real. It's not just some idea or goal that floated through your head while you were making a sandwich. It's a written promise to yourself that you're going to do anything and everything you can to get there.

Goal examples:

- Become student body president
- Become fluent in Spanish
- Study abroad in Spain
- Receive the communications scholarship
- Start a blog

Use the following chart to help you. You can also look at my chart as an example. Remember, these charts mean nothing without action.

It's not about what we dream … it's about what we do when we wake up.

Wake up and smell the coffee, my friends.

Goal 1: Start *Headbands of Hope*				
Strategies to get there	Action Steps	What resources do you have to help?	Completion Date	
			Estimated	Actual
Create a business plan	• Meet with a Business professor • Get a business license	• The Business School • Entrepreneur Club • Talk to Dad about license	1/1/12	1/15/12
Find a supplier	• Meet with Textile School • Draw up designs	• Textile professors • Talk to girl in Eng 101 class about designs	3/1/12	4/1/12
Get HoH launch on university website	• Find person who works website • Write up press release	• Talk to Student Ambassador Director • Go to Admissions Office and ask • Have professor proofread my press release	4/25/12	4/15/12

Now it's your turn:

Goal 1:				
Strategies to get there	Action Steps	What resources do you have to help?	Completion Date	
			Estimated	Actual

Goal 2:				
Strategies to get there	Action Steps	What resources do you have to help?	Completion Date	
			Estimated	Actual

Goal 3:				
Strategies to get there	Action Steps	What resources do you have to help?	Completion Date	
			Estimated	Actual

Acknowledgements

First off, I'd like to thank my second grade teacher, Mrs. Deal, for pulling my ticket for talking too much during reading time. You taught me that being put in line isn't the end of the world and needs to be done … and you also taught me my vowels, which was a biggie too.

I'd like to thank Dr. Maria De Moya for volunteering your time to mentor me as a student at NC State. You taught me about PR and communications, but the biggest lesson you taught me was goal setting.

I'd like to thank Dean Phillips for writing my letter of recommendation to be the commencement speaker at NC State Graduation. Because of you, twenty thousand people got to hear my message.

I'd like to thank Mindy Sopher for being the sweetest, caring and strongest person I know. Because of you, I'm constantly reminded I have choices in my life. My first choice will always be to have you around!

I'd like to thank NC State University for accepting me into college … despite my SAT scores. And I'd like to thank you for always encouraging your students to challenge the status quo and think innovatively. When I got the idea for Headbands of Hope my sophomore year, I knew I had the resources and support at NC State to make it happen.

I'd like to thank CAMPUSPEAK for being the first to believe in me as an inspirational speaker. Because of you, I get to inspire thousands of students with my story every month.

Lisa Friedman, thank you for making this book a reality. You have been an amazing mentor and friend. I promise I'll do what you asked when I'm fifty ... or fifty-four.

Thank you to my wonderful contributors in this book: Katelynn, Amber, Kate, Mari Ann, Karly, Stacy, Emily, Amanda, Lauren and Tammy. And thank you to Lauren Hadeed for the amazing cover design!

Heather, thank you for letting me travel vicariously through you. When you send me pictures of you in Alaska running from a bear, I feel like I'm there with you. Thank you for being the best big sister and always trying things out before me ... like the high beam at gymnastics ... or vegetables.

Jake, thank you for dealing with my craziness ... and watching *The Bachelorette* with me on Monday nights. Wait—should I not say that in public?

Mom, thank you for always being my number one cheerleader. You always make me believe that no dream is too big. After Heather and I won first place with our five-star performance of *Hello Mudda Hello Fadda* at the Cornelius Elementary talent show, I knew you were right: hard work makes dreams come true.

Camper, thank you for being the best dog in the world. I swear, you are human.

Dad, thank you for not getting mad at me for selling you and mom's stuff on eBay when I was 12. I always wondered why I didn't get in trouble, and now I realize it's because you saw an entrepreneurial spirit in me.

Love,
Jess

About Jess Ekstrom

During her junior year of college, Jess started her own company, Headbands of Hope, to help brighten the lives of children battling cancer. She's been featured in *Forbes, Entrepreneur*, NBC's *TODAY Show* and more. But more importantly, she was able to help thousands of girls by the time she graduated from North Carolina State University in May 2013. Today, Jess is a full-time CEO and motivational speaker for college students.

In her spare time, Jess enjoys watching (and playing) football, going on adventures, spending time with friends and family, and helping others find their path to make a difference.

Twitter/Instagram:
@HeadbandsofHope
@Jlekstro

Facebook:
/headbandsofhope
/jessekstrom

Send a picture of you reading the book using the hashtag #TFF for a
chance to win a copy for your friends!
For feedback:
www.TheFreshmanFabulous.com

For speaking inquiries:
www.JessEkstrom.com

For awesome headbands:
www.HeadbandsOfHope.org

Thank you for reading!
Stay fun, stay curious, stay ambitious, stay fabulous.